BEACH WALKING IN SAN DIEGO COUNTY

II

Beach Walking in San Diego County

by
William Carroll

First Edition

Printed in the United States of America
ISBN 0-910390-33-9
Library of Congress Catalog Card Number: 91-73239

Coda Publications
P.O. Bin 711
San Marcos, California 92079-0711

For those great conservationists who fight so
hard to maintain our ocean frontage in its
delightfully uninhibited state.

Contents

"We all grow older but we do not have to become old"

The Relationship Book

Beach Walking in San Diego County

It has never been easier to explore and enjoy beaches, marinas, water-front parks, tidepools and the wondrous salt evaporation ponds of San Diego's coastline and bays.

Credit goes to Southern California's mild climate which usually succeeds in making waterfront activities a constant enjoyment. To enhance your pleasure, here's a guidebook for years of valued use because *Beach Walking in San Diego County* details over 100 miles of ocean coast and bay waterfront. Included is: How to get there with car or public transportation, parking availability and what you'll find on arrival.

Recreational opportunities range from wonderful miles-long ocean-beach walks paced to the music of breaking Pacific waves to easy-going paved walkway strolls past shade trees, benches and frequent opportunities for refreshment. For family picnic planning you will find that details of each area may include: BBQs, picnic tables, restrooms, showers, telephones, fire rings, children's playgrounds and similar facilities.

Although this guidebook covers only waterfront recreation, other books in the series reveal more of the County. *Park Walking in San Diego County* provides the details of 384 public parks including several each in Temecula and El Centro. A companion volume, *Mall Walking in San Diego County*, is the guide to recreational activities that may be enjoyed in the County's malls and shopping centers. Included are over a hundred measured walks, plus maps of the larger malls. Both *Park* and *Mall Walking* include basic information on how to get there, parking, restrooms, telephones, picnic facilities, playgrounds and opportunities for family recreation or exercise walking.

Beach Walking in San Diego County

In this book, *Beach Walking in San Diego County*, there are over 50 user-friendly strip maps. They reveal every inch of the Pacific Ocean coast and San Diego bay fronts, from the Orange County line on the north to our nation's border with Mexico on the south. Each strip map has been simplified to essentials of the easiest route to a desired waterfront site. In addition, both waterfront sites and destination routes are keyed to specific pages and grid locations of the *Thomas Street Guide and Directory* for San Diego County. With that definitive work as a reference, finding a specific ocean or bay beach, park or marina will be less troublesome.

Public transportation by bus or trolley has been identified by coach number. The transit district's telephone number is included as a source of schedule and fare information. Parking facilities are described and directions to unusual or confusing entrances have been provided. Restroom availability keystones the listing of site facilities which may include such amenities as: BBQs, fire rings, picnic tables, children's playgrounds, grass, shade, water fountains and showers. Site jurisdiction is listed with a telephone number for additional usage information.

Beaches are described as sand, pebbles (which are often walkable) and rocky. The latter waterfront areas are not recommended for either walking or water-based recreation. Lifeguard towers are listed in locations where they have been found. Many beaches are noted for their surfing potential and others for a tidepool collection worthy of exploration. Each type of additional pleasure potential has been included in these pages.

Many beaches and parking lots have specified hours for public use. When known, these open hours have been added to *Beach Walking in San Diego County*. The liberal use of photographs shows the great variety of typical waterfront activity sites in the County. Several pages of text highlight the history of Camp Pendleton which operates on land of the original 89,742-acre Santa Margarita y Las Flores Grant of 1830.

Final pages include a carefully compiled cross-index which makes it possible to find every waterfront site by its common name, it's proper or dedicated name and by area of location. As additional assistance, city beaches have been listed under their municipal jurisdiction. You will also find the telephone number of the City Recreation Department for additional information. Many beaches and beachfront parks have special areas which can be reserved for use by family or group parties.

Beach Walking in San Diego County

A telephone call to the jurisdiction involved will provide details for such use. Reserved areas range in size from small to those adequate for groups of thousands. The greatest number of such special areas are located around Mission Bay.

Few waterfront recreational sites have direction signs of importance. For on-site information look for a guard tower or youth with a surfboard. The latter usually know the most about their local beach and can be helpful in advising of the best swimming locations or points of view to watch surfing at its best.

Beach walking is totally different from park or mall walking. Coastal waterfronts are constantly changing as weather affects tides and wave action. What may be a pebble beach this year could well be covered with fine sand by next. Exploration is the name of the best fun; all of which is within minutes of San Diego County's most populous locations.

Availability of food at a waterfront site varies from "nothing" to some of the County's finest restaurants. For example; in Cardiff-by-the-Sea there are fine ocean beaches on both sides of a number of equally fine restaurants. At the Embarcadero of the City of San Diego there is no sand but the finest of viewpoints for watching ocean-going ship activity in San Diego Bay: Plus a vast number of the City's best dining establishments. Each of this book's site-listings contains information on potential sources of food or beverages.

Within *Beach Walking in San Diego County* you will find many fine recreational and walking sites worth visiting. This book's detailed information on how to get there, what you will find on arrival, and suggestions for exercise, recreation or picnics makes it easy to plan ahead with confidence and pleasure.

Beach Walking in San Diego County

Walking and Health

Beaches, nature's grandest attraction, have been a constant delight since man began with their the never-ending rhythm of breaking waves and seductive sand under warming sun. Of all California, San Diego County offers the greatest variety of Pacific Ocean recreation. From the famous surfing beaches of San Onofre and Swami's, to the picturesque sand and mysterious caves of La Jolla, there is something for everyone.

Beach-walking preparation is almost non-existent and equipment may range from no-cost bare feet to expensive water-tolerant walking shoes. Though the majority of sites in *Beach Walking in San Diego County* are sand beaches, there are a number of pebble shores where walking requires great care but, as a reward, provides more exercise. A small number of local beaches are rocky and scrambling over wet or mossed rocks could lead to a hurtful fall. In some areas astounding cliffs sheer down to the waves and coast walking is only possible at low tide.

For family recreation, a beach is considered perfection. There are often fire rings and at some beach sites you will find BBQs, picnic tables and children's playgrounds. All of which add to ocean swimming and sand castles as an ideal excursion site.

Waterfront watching is offered in a wondrous variety of sites along the bays of San Diego. The man-made Mission Bay recreation area, is bordered by grassed parks, sand beaches and complete facilities. On some Bay waters jet-skis swoosh past, in other areas there will be sailing craft, power boats or water ski enthusiasts. There is also a huge Mission Bay model-yacht pond where miniature boats are raced by their enthusiastic owners.

Beach Walking in San Diego County

Along the Embarcadero, at the feet of the City of San Diego, huge ocean liners and ships of the Navy's Pacific Fleet majestically glide to and from the mouth of San Diego Bay at Point Loma. South of the Embarcadero is Tuna Harbor where commercial fishing boats unload and are maintained in the traditional manner. Nearby ship repair yards bulge with huge floating dry-docks holding vessels undergoing reconstruction. Even further south are acres of evaporation ponds from which sea salt is reclaimed and shipped all over the United States.

It seems that marinas are everywhere. Open to public inspection; they hold a mind-boggling collection of private craft. These range from ocean-going yachts of unbelievable size and cost to tiny dinghies scuttling from dock to deck like wandering sea fowl. Adjacent to many marinas, and scattered along the coast, are magnificent public parks overlooking the Pacific. Here are picnic facilities for family outings and park benches strategically placed to watch colorful sunsets drop below the horizon.

From all of these, there are walking routes worthy of venture. For newcomers to the nation's most popular form of exercise a good level of health-supporting activity is said to be about 30 minutes of moderately fast walking four times a week. Should you be overweight, walk for a longer period of time and eat less until the weight problem is minimal and your body chemistry becomes balanced. Medical reports indicate that a body in good condition does a better job of using its food intake than does a body in poor condition. This is considered to be another indication that a healthy body gains less from the meal that would add unwanted pounds onto a body less functional.

It was also reported that about three months of consistent vigorous exercise will bring almost any useful body up to its reasonable peak. Many health enthusiasts work out in a gym or spa to build muscles, jog or run and gain wind, or lift weights to enhance what they are able to raise off the ground. Generally speaking, these are add-ons to being in good physical condition. In early stages of walking your way to better health the values of feeling better and being more in control of your body are the initial, and most important, benefits of such exercise.

It is worth pointing out that when you plan any walking venture to be a vigorous workout, begin with five or ten minutes of slow walking to warm the body to its new task., Once warmed up, consider walking a mile in about 15 minutes. This equals four miles an hour which is considered a fairly rapid pace over soft sand and a reasonable walk on harder surfaces. The secret to making this an maximum-effort walk is a full swing of the arms with every step. In effect, this adds upper body exercise to benefits usually reserved for legs,lungs and heart. The arm-waving technique should be practiced for short distances over a period of several walking ventures while building up to its con-tinual use for a full mile. You may meet walkers who have added one or two weights to their wrists, or carry plastic containers of water in each hand, as additions to the workout factor. It is es-timated that they gain four or five percent more benefit from their workout by adding such weight.

One special need for beach-walkers is to walk in both directions during each outing because beaches slope down to the water. Walking only in one direction will keep the hips tilted higher up on one side. Walking in both directions will give the hips an equal dose of exercise in alternative positions and eliminate discomfort that often results from long-time unequal positioning of the body's skeletal structure.

When possible arrange to walk with a partner or group. Comparisons and challenges add pleasure to the venture be-cause friends will often cause you to exercise a bit harder than you might push by yourself. All of which adds up to a greater measure of improved overall health.

As you walk with others you will notice as many pos-tures as there are walkers. How you upgrade your body could begin with standing comfortably erect to raise the rib cage and give your lungs the maximum amount of space within which to expand. Then maintain your shoulders back and level by noting where the thumbs touch your thighs. Unless your arms are grossly unequal, or you are standing on a beach slope, the thumbs should be in about the same place on each side. A fur-ther improvement in posture will come from pulling your stomach in and thrusting the hip joints forward to set the spine in a near vertical position. This tends to eliminate the so-called 'swayback' which causes many complaints of aching back.

Swing your arms naturally and use a normal length step while warming up. After the five-minute warm-up, begin swing-ing your legs forward and striding out as far as is comfortable. This striding-out technique exercises muscles with a bit of gentle stretching. It also allows the hip joints a chance to ex-plore new territory and reduce their aches and pains from the stiffness of inaction. Move each foot well out, put it down on the heel, roll the foot forward and pick up cleanly. Practice an aggressive walking technique with the same attention you would give the game of golf. Then, when postured walking becomes so natural you no longer think about it, take a good look at yourself in a store window as you stroll past. The new image of a healthy well-figured person becomes all the reward you will need.

There appears to be very little difference between health benefits from exercise walking as compared to operating a treadmill or stair-step device. It simply boils down to how long you walk, whether uphill or down, and slow or fast: Plus how convenient it is to exercise when and where.

Shoe selection for beach walking is not as complicated as selecting shoes for hiking or mountain walking. The first requirement for beach walking is that the shoe upper be of a man-made fabric which is tolerant of salt water and can be rinsed in tap water. Additionally, the fabric should breathe to keep your feet cool during hot summer days. And without question: The shoe must be comfortable to the entire foot. A top-quality shoe, such as shown on the next page, will be less expensive in the long run and provide maximum support for your hard-working feet. There's little problem in finding the proper last for it's said there are over 200 different models of sport shoes. Some manufacturers produce men's and women's shoes in widths from AAAA. to EE. and in sizes 4 to 14.

For sand-beach walking, a flexible sole will give your feet the greatest amount of exercise. A lightweight upper, which laces high up the ankle, provides maximum support and will assist in maintaining balance should you step into a hole or trip in a washed area. If you have a tendency to wear a shoe's sole off to either side, it is one sign that ankle-high tops are needed to support your ankles and straighten your footstep.

On the other hand, if your beaches are both sand and pebbles, your shoe should have a moderately firm outer sole and cushioned inner sole to protect delicate foot bones from the continual impact of the variety of surfaces found along a shore. The best outer sole will be sufficiently firm to protect the foot from unexpected pressure points of sharp objects hidden in the water. Wide deep grooves in the sole provide maximum non-skid traction on wet rocks and over moist growths.

Typical high-tech walking shoes have features similar to this New Balance model which demonstrates advanced technology to promote walking efficiency.

Padded tongue and quarter lining provide a comfortable wearing surface.

A firm saddle area is important for mid-foot support.

Soft fabric uppers present a fine appearance and many are perforated for breathability. Man-made fabrics dry most rapidly and pass additional cooling air.

A modern inside vamp lining wicks moisture from the foot.

The midsole must be firm to maintain stability yet be flexible to make walking easy. Multi-density midsoles often have a soft heel pad for cushioning and a firm arch area to efficiently translate the walker's body-weight to the forefoot.

The molded counter portion of the footbed rolls upward at the sides and rear to keep the foot in place. An extended reinforcement maintains structural integrity of the shoe while stabilizing the mid- and rear-foot area.

Inclusion of a metatarsal pad increases forefoot flexibility.

A heel insert assists in forward-motion transfer of leg and body weight from the point of heel strike to lift off for the next step.

An abrasion-resisting outsole should be of semi-hard material with ridging, or lug-pattern tread design, for good traction. Dual-density outsoles can provide protection from sharp objects and additional cushioning for the feet.

Beach Walking in San Diego County

It is worth keeping mind that while high shoes offer better support they are heavier, about which more later. Low shoes may be easier to walk in but provide the least support. A good compromise is the well-designed walking shoe with a collar which fits snugly below the ankle and is sufficiently flexible to be comfortable.

For sure bring or buy a pair of thick walking socks, of artificial-fabric, to wear while trying on new shoes: Otherwise you could end up with shoes that will be much too tight when put to hard use. To begin with, make sure the shape of the shoe you are considering matches the shape of your foot. When standing in the laced shoe, insist on from 1/3rd to 1/2-inch of space between your big toe and end of the shoe. If the area over the toe is high, and there is plenty of room between your toenail and interior of the shoe, that is a plus. A soft roll around the top of the shoe, with an extension pad up the back, can be good or bad depending on fit of the shoe and what feels most comfortable to you. A well-fitting upper must lace to a snug fit around the entire foot to keep it from sliding inside the shoe when soaked with water or gaining blisters from walking rapidly on hot sand.

The best informative fitting test is a fast and hard walkabout inside the store in shoes you are planning to buy. This is a good way to be reasonably sure their areas of flexibility and stiffness are harmonious with the manner in which your feet are most comfortable while walking. The best beach-walking shoe will have a sole which is flexible enough to bend naturally forward from the moment you plant your heel until you move forward and lift the toe area to take another step. Poor shoes could quickly become painful and inhibit your pleasure.

There are two final points to consider: One is shoe weight. You will pick them up and lay them down many thousands of times during a day's walk. The less they weigh the easier walking is. On the other hand a heavy shoe gives your muscles more of a workout.

The second point is flexibility. A soft shoe that is too flexible provides little assistance to control your stride. A stiff shoe provides extra stride control but may feel like a Dutch wooden clog. Try to find shoes demonstrating a comfortable balance between soft and firm, with a bit of bias toward more firm than less. The best shoe makes you feel secure while walking over the many surfaces likely to be found along a waterfront.

Beach recreation during most Southern California seasons calls for the minimum investment in clothing. While bikinis do well when an overall suntan is desired, for serious exercise walking your clothing should begin with underwear of polyester or polypropylene. These artificial fabrics allow natural body moisture to pass through and evaporate, which helps keep your body at its normal temperature. Cotton is comfortable but tends to hold moisture and become soggy. Outerwear could be a simple sweat suit to keep you as warm as you like. Loose-fitting tropical clothing allows you to enjoy being a bit on the cool side and is best on a blinding hot day. A light jacket would be a colorful identifier and enough protection for that memory-laden final walk while the sun is setting and ocean breezes are cooling.

During inclement weather, when beach-walking is at its most exciting, the more closely you maintain normal body temperature the better your walk will be. Wear good quality thermal underwear made of an artificial fabric to pass and evaporate body moisture. Pants, shorts and sweaters should maintain warmth and be worn in layers as the temperature dictates. A good jacket with weatherproof nylon outer surfaces is desirable.

In almost all seasons, a headcovering is welcome at beaches or waterfronts. When the sun is skin-burning hot the hat will protect you from skin damage and dulled hair. During cold weather or foggy days the head covering will shed excess moisture and help you to remain warm. In short, be comfortable.

When you are involved in a multi-mile beach walk, plan ahead to maintain your energy at a useful level instead of fighting the highs and lows associated with heavy spread-out meals. A light breakfast when you walk early will allow brunching at ten or eleven. Or brunch first, then walk the noon hours away. Break longer walks with a tea or lemonade stop to rest the body and replace lost fluids. Carrying a walker's bottle on your belt loop, filled with water or beverage, is easy. Most sports stores have a wide selection of such bottles to choose from. If you snack while exercising, select carbohydrates and leave fatty, protein-rich meals for social gatherings and appreciation of mother's home cooking. One bit of good diet news which surfaced recently indicated that mild exercise, like walking, greatly improved the body's beneficial use of protein. In effect, with regular exercise you may be able to enjoy a greater variety of tasty foods with less damage to your vitality or bathroom scale.

Beach Walking in San Diego County

According to the *Wellness Letter*, published by the University of California at Berkeley, being continually active is the key to weight control and good health for an average person. Burning 1000 calories a week in moderate activity is the *Letter's* basic recommendation for health-giving exercise. Normal physical condition being considered, age appears to be of little importance., Reasonable activity has been shown to improve mobility and strength for individuals 80 and 90 years of age. Neck stiffness, back pain, and headaches have long been known to become less a problem during and following regular exercise programs. A reduction of stress and improved cardiovascular performance are believed to be responsible for the decrease in such uncomfortable common problems.

Not to mention that regular exercise has long been known to help us all live better and enjoy more.

Which is what *Beach Walking in San Diego County* is all about: Living better. No matter where you are in the County, it is only a short distance to the ocean or bay front. It's even possible that a schedule of regular exercise would feel so good that you would make it a part of your lifestyle. From then on it's all for the good: Fewer problems with weight control, better general health and more new friends with similar objectives.

As American's most popular recreational activity, walking is today's way to go.

Beach Walking in San Diego County

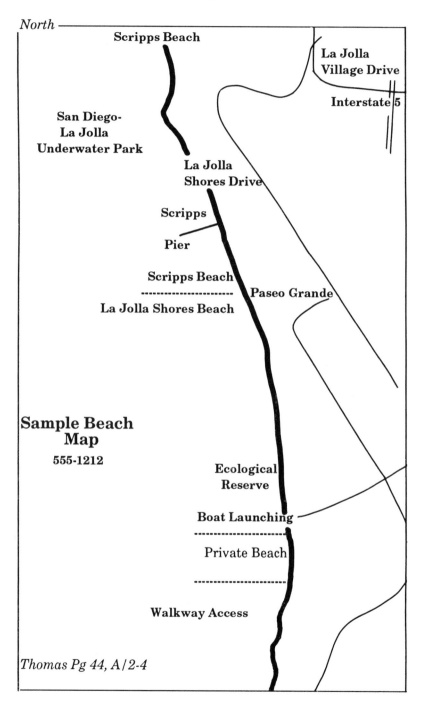

Beach Walking in San Diego County

Sample Map Page

A typical access route is described somewhat as follows:

This beach area is reached off Interstate 5 via the La Jolla Village Drive offramp (Pg 44, C/2). Drive west to North Torrey Pines Road. Turn right then make a quick left onto La Jolla Shores Drive (Pg 44, B/2). Look for Paseo Grande (Pg 44, A/3) on the right as you pass Scripps Institution of Oceanography.

Most major route instructions begin with exiting from Interstate 5 which is the primary North-South freeway in San Diego County. The exit ramps are keyed to the *Thomas Guide* by page number *(Pg 44)* and by grid location *(C/2)* on the *Thomas Guide* notations at the top of this page. Notes at the bottom of the map page on the left refer to the general location of listed sites.

On the map at the left beaches, parks and other waterfront features are identified by their general location. Though the waterfront is an accurate rendition of the area, many features; spread up and down the coast for some distance.

The telephone number below a beach is that of the jurisdiction.

The dotted line extending from the waterfront denotes a boundary between two jurisdictions. A good example is the small private beach between the Boat Launching ramp and the Walkway Access.

<u>These maps are not to scale</u> as to road and highway locations. Only recommended routes are shown. To simplify the presentation, minor streets or highways are not always included. For complete details of the area it is well to review the site as located by *Thomas Guide* data in the map's lower left corner.

Beach characteristics often change from season to season, depending on tide and weather/storm conditions. Do not be surprised if a beach listed as 'pebbles' is covered with fine sand or a sand beach has been temporarily eroded to base material.

Tide/Temperature information is available from 221-8881. The emergency telephone number for lifeguard services is 911.

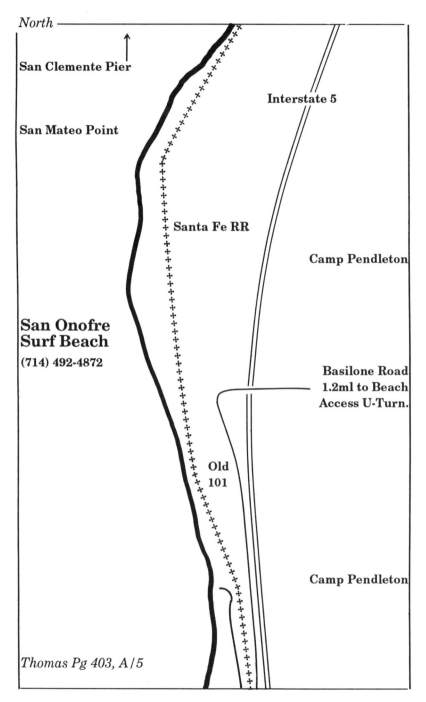

North

San Clemente Pier

San Mateo Point

Interstate 5

Santa Fe RR

Camp Pendleton

San Onofre
Surf Beach
(714) 492-4872

Basilone Road
1.2ml to Beach
Access U-Turn.

Old
101

Camp Pendleton

Thomas Pg 403, A/5

Beach Walking in San Diego County

From Interstate 5, use the Basilone Road (*Pg 403, A/5*) offramp, turn toward the ocean, follow Old Highway 101 south 1.4 miles to a blue 'Beach Access - Parking Lot 4' sign. Turn right, then right again as 'Beach Access' signs direct. Within .8 mile turn left into San Onofre Surf Beach. (Entry fee) There is a parking lot on the left as you enter and about .8 mile of parking along the beach-front drive. No public transportation or food.

The 1.4ml of Surf Beach is open from 0600 to 2200. The area is patrolled by park police and lifeguard towers are on the beach which is under control of the State of California. The north end of Surf Beach is a wide sand area suitable for swimming. The south end is narrow, covered with large pebbles and provides some of California's best surfing. There are numerous rest rooms, cold showers, running water, picnic tables, BBQs, fire rings and limited shade. A public telephone is available near the centrally located restroom. For information telephone (714) 492-4872.   Lifeguard emergency (714) 492-5171 or Dial 911.

The water front is walkable for about four miles in either direction: North to San Clemente Pier and south to the Camp Pendleton fence beyond which passage is not permitted.

To reach the San Onofre Beach Campground area (*Pg 403, B/6*), which has splendid beaches, do not follow 'Beach Access' signs to Surf Beach. Instead; continue south on Old Highway 101 toward the San Onofre Nuclear Station (*Pg 403, A/5*). About one-half mile past the Station guardhouse you will arrive at the Campground kiosk (Entry fee), First Aid Station and carlot.

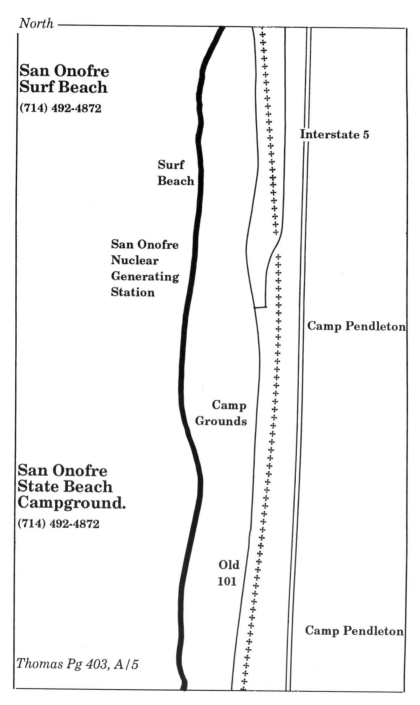

North

**San Onofre
Surf Beach**

(714) 492-4872

**Surf
Beach**

Interstate 5

**San Onofre
Nuclear
Generating
Station**

Camp Pendleton

**Camp
Grounds**

**San Onofre
State Beach
Campground.**

(714) 492-4872

**Old
101**

Camp Pendleton

Thomas Pg 403, A/5

Beach Walking in San Diego County

Thomas Guide
Pg 403, A/5

San Onofre Nuclear Station
San Onofre Beach Campground

Shortly after Old 101 bridges the railway tracks you will find blue signs on the right directing you to 'Parking Lot 4 - Beach Access'. This is the road to Surf Beach but do not follow these "Beach Access" signs to reach the Campground. See route below.

To reach the San Onofre Beach Campground area (*Pg 403, B/6*), which also has miles of splendid beaches, do not follow the 'Beach Access' signs to Surf Beach. Instead; continue south on Old Highway 101 toward the San Onofre Nuclear Station (*Pg 403, A/5*). About one-half mile past the Station guardhouse you will arrive at the Campground entrance kiosk (Entry fee), First Aid Station and vehicle parking areas. Open 0600-2000.

The Nuclear Generating Station (*Pg 403, A/5*) is located on government land leased for 60-years. In 1964 the utility operators agreed to pay the U.S. $91,291 per year for use of the 84-acre site. The $87 million plant was completed and dedicated in 1967. Visitor tours may be arranged from (714) 458-4631.

Beach Walking in San Diego County

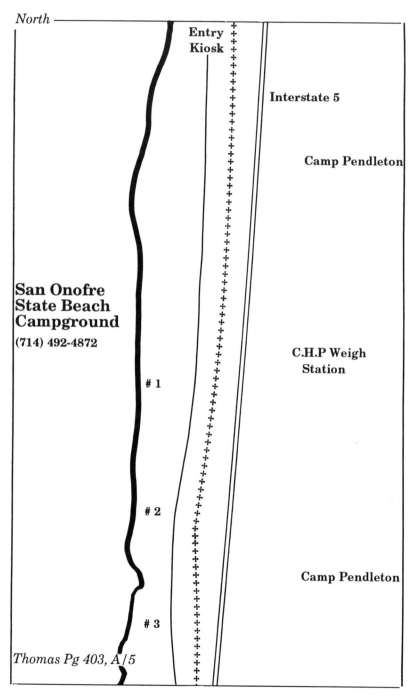

North ──────

Entry
Kiosk

Interstate 5

Camp Pendleton

**San Onofre
State Beach
Campground**

(714) 492-4872

1

C.H.P Weigh
Station

2

Camp Pendleton

3

Thomas Pg 403, A/5

Beach Walking in San Diego County

San Onofre Beach Campground

San Onofre State Beach and Public Campground (*Pg 403, B / 6*) is open from 0600 to 2200 daily. Overnight tent camping, RV parking, and day use are subject to fee permits. The Ranger at the entry kiosk (First Aid) can provide directions to the day-use carlot. A nearby trail leads to the Echo Arch campground area and down to the adjacent beach. A public telephone is near the kiosk. Food supplies are available but no public transportation.

The area is patrolled by park police and lifeguard towers are on the beach. Though the area is a portion of Camp Pendleton, it is leased to the State of California for public recreational use. For beach and campground information, telephone (714) 492-4872. For Lifeguard emergency service (714) 492-5171 or Dial 911.

Restrooms, cold-water showers, sources of running water and public telephones are along the ocean side of Old 101. Camping and parking spaces are assigned and clearly marked. There are picnic tables and BBQs or fire rings near most of the spaces.

Trail # 1 is an easy walk to the sand beach. It connects with the Echo Arch Loop Trail and campground. A restroom is nearby.

This is one of the better beaches in San Diego County. It is over eight miles long from Camp Pendleton's fence on the south to the San Clemente Pier on the north.

Trail # 2 leads directly down to the sand beach and guard towers. There are two Trailhead entrances, one on either side of the adjacent restroom.

There are cold-water showers at each restroom. The camp parking area is patrolled and a 15 MPH speed limit enforced.

Trail # 3 leads to a sand beach and tidepools which are best explored at low tide. A restroom at the Trailhead has a public telephone. There is another restroom between Trail # 3 and Trail # 4. Trailhead signs are by the roadside.

Beach Walking in San Diego County

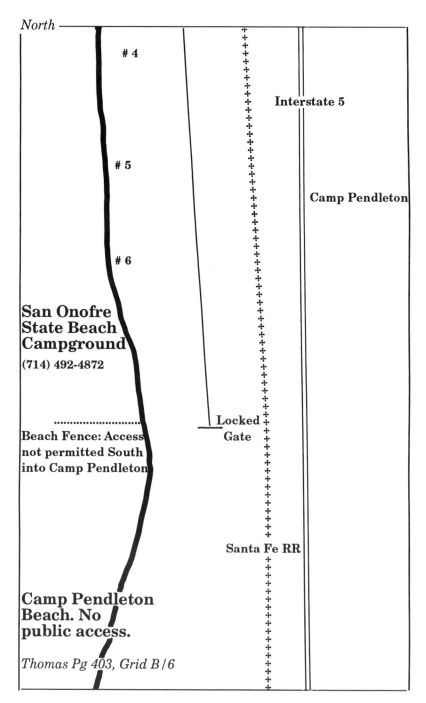

North

4

Interstate 5

5

Camp Pendleton

6

**San Onofre
State Beach
Campground**
(714) 492-4872

Locked
Gate

**Beach Fence: Access
not permitted South
into Camp Pendleton**

Santa Fe RR

**Camp Pendleton
Beach. No
public access.**

Thomas Pg 403, Grid B/6

Beach Walking in San Diego County

Thomas Guide
Pg 403, B / 6

San Onofre Beach Campground

Trail # 4 is an easy walk to the sand beach. The area is recommended for surf fishing. There is a restroom with cold-water showers and running water between Trailhead # 4 and # 5.

Trail # 5 is described as "challenging". The Trailhead is located near a restroom with cold-water showers and running water.

Trail # 6 begins near a restroom with cold-water showers, running water and public telephone. This is an attractive walk down to the sand beach although the return is steep.

The south limits of San Onofre State Beach are marked by a wire fence at the boundary with Camp Pendleton. Beach walking is not allowed past the fence line. In the Campground area, on the bluff, the pavement of Old 101 is barred by a locked gate at the south end. Only bicycle riders are permitted past the gate.

Beach Walking in San Diego County

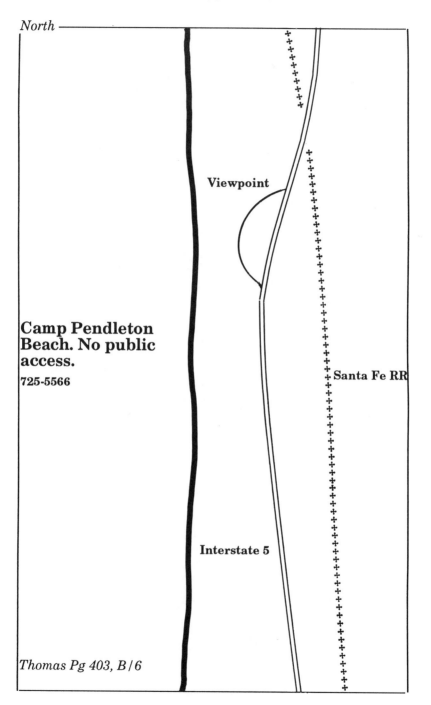

North

Viewpoint

Camp Pendleton Beach. No public access.
725-5566

Santa Fe RR

Interstate 5

Thomas Pg 403, B/6

Beach Walking in San Diego County

Thomas Guide Pg 403, B/6   **Camp Pendleton Beach**

The Viewpoint (*Pg 403,B/6*), on the west side of Interstate 5, has no services or facilities. It is managed by CalTrans, 688-6670. The area is fenced and there is no access to Camp Pendleton. Walking is limited to the enclosed Viewpoint site. The nearest restrooms are six miles south at the Aliso Rest Stop.

Camp Pendleton was originally Santa Margarita y Las Flores, a portion of land controlled by San Luis Rey Mission. In 1830 the Mexican government took most mission land and left the priests only small areas actively used for support of mission residents.

Shortly afterward the Mexican governor granted 89,742 acres of what is now Camp Pendleton to Pio Pico, an administrator of mission lands. Pico added 43,698 acres for a grand total of 133,440 acres. He controlled 20 miles of coastline, owned three lakes and the water of seven rivers. Current U.S. Geographic maps refer to the area as the Santa Margarita y Las Flores Grant. At its greatest, it totaled 335 square miles, was about one-quarter the size of the State of Rhode Island and extended north from Oceanside to El Toro.

Pico had the Santa Margarita adobe ranch house built on his property. In an expanded form, the adobe is now used by Camp Pendleton's Commandant as his residence. About 15 years after accepting the Grant, Pico became insolvent and sold his property to John Forster for $14,000. When Forster died in 1881, the property was sold to Richard O'Neill who was backed by San Francisco financier James Flood. The price was $250,000 and assumption of a $207,000 mortgage: About $3.40 an acre.

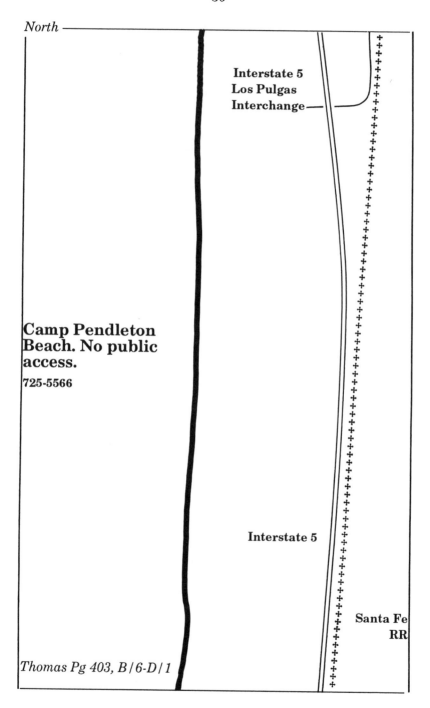

North

Interstate 5
Los Pulgas
Interchange

Camp Pendleton
Beach. No public
access.
725-5566

Interstate 5

Santa Fe
RR

Thomas Pg 403, B / 6-D / 1

Beach Walking in San Diego County

Thomas Guide Pg 403, B/6, D/1 **Camp Pendleton Beach**

Las Pulgas Road (*Pg 403, B/6*) interchange serves only Camp Pendleton. Beach and area access is strictly controlled.

A few hundred yards south-east of this exit from Interstate 5 are ruins of the Asistencia de Las Flores. The Asistencia was built in the early 1800s by Mission San Luis Rey indians as a rest and remount station for travelers between Mission San Juan Capistrano and Mission San Luis Rey. At one time there was a small ranch house on Los Flores Creek, near the Asistencia. It was occupied by tenant-farmers and friends of the O'Neills.

O'Neill's objective was to turn the Santa Margarita into a profitable cattle ranch. By 1882 he was busy expanding the ranch house and buying herds of cattle. He also had agreed to the intrusion of train tracks between Oceanside and Fallbrook on condition there was a flag stop near the ranch house.

The train operated on a comfortable schedule. It left Fallbrook in the morning, stopped at the Santa Margarita for passengers and continued to Oceanside. From there it ran to Vista, San Marcos and Escondido. After a lunch layover it was headed back to Oceanside and the Santa Margarita to conclude its run in Fallbrook. During hunting season the crew often parked the train by a ranch lake while they shot wild fowl for dinner.

O'Neill established *vaquero* camps on San Onofre Creek, at San Mateo, Los Pulgas ('The Fleas') and at Mission Viejo. His men worked out from the four sites to track herds, repair fences and maintain sources of water. Rodeos were usually at San Mateo near the railroad siding. At that time a 'rodeo' was when cattle were herded to a central point for inspection by cattle buyers from San Diego, Los Angeles and San Francisco. 'Brandings' were held at the vaquero camp nearest the herd to be branded.

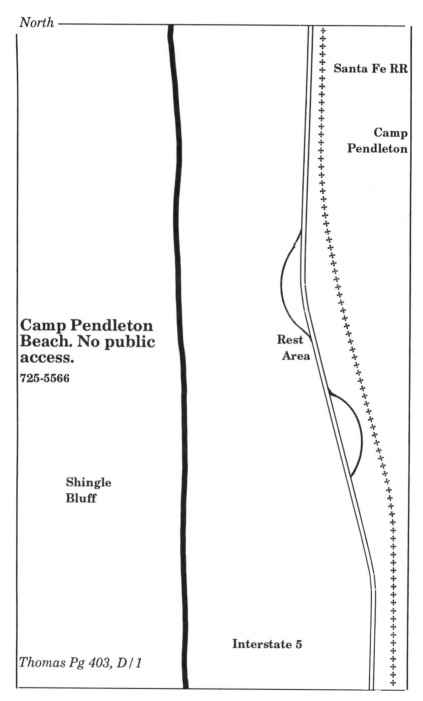

North

Santa Fe RR

Camp
Pendleton

Camp Pendleton
Beach. No public
access.

725-5566

Rest
Area

Shingle
Bluff

Interstate 5

Thomas Pg 403, D / 1

Beach Walking in San Diego County

Thomas Guide Pg 403, D/1　　**Camp Pendleton Beach**

The Aliso Rest Area (*Pg 403, D/1*) has restrooms, telephones, picnic tables, some shade and a play area. Mobile food services are often found in the large parking lot. The area is fenced and there is no access onto surrounding Camp Pendleton beach or land. The Aliso Rest Area is managed by CalTrans, 688-6670.

Pico's original adobe ranch house was expanded to a traditional Mexican hacienda with a park-like center square surrounded by living quarters. A unique feature was the ranch's first running water: To the kitchen and garden. Other users filled their pitcher from a barrel by the kitchen door. Nearby was the three-person adobe outhouse. Inside was a large seat for men, a medium size seat for ladies and a small seat for children. The two smaller seats had steps to accommodate diminished heights of the users. Further distant from the ranch house was the *vaquero's* bunkhouse, a blacksmith shop and the horsebarn.

Demise of the Santa Margarita began September 8, 1939, when President Franklin D. Roosevelt proclaimed a "State of Limited National Emergency" based on Europe's upheaval. The army immediately initiated a search for West Coast training acreage. Their early report termed the ranch as "Too far from San Diego".

Nevertheless, in March of 1941, U.S. Army representatives met with owners of the Santa Margarita who offered to sell the ranch for $4.5 million or lease it for $3.50 an acre per year. Negotiations were continuing when Roosevelt declared a "State of Unlimited National Emergency". The Navy reacted by purchasing 9000 acres near Fallbrook for an ammunition depot.

Beach Walking in San Diego County

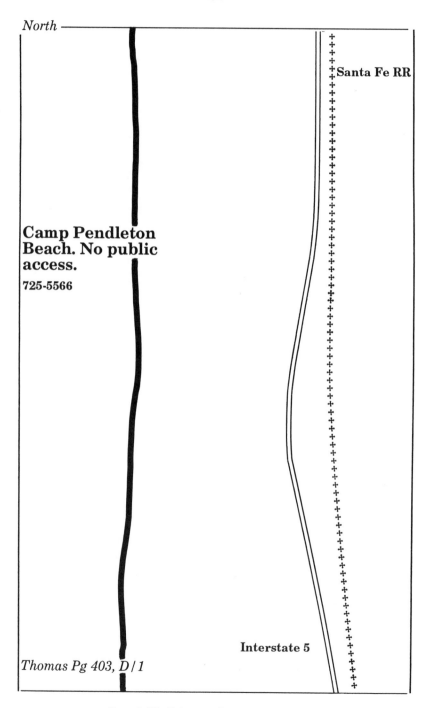

North

Santa Fe RR

Camp Pendleton Beach. No public access.

725-5566

Interstate 5

Thomas Pg 403, D / 1

Beach Walking in San Diego County

Pearl Harbor justified immediate action and the Army promptly decided the Santa Margarita was too rugged for training armored divisions. The Marine Corps jumped from the sidelines, used the Army's research as a foundation and on February 27, 1942, issued a requisition for the ranch. It was promptly approved by the office of the Secretary of the Navy. In March the site was named Camp Joseph H. Pendleton to honor a highly regarded retired Marine General and Mayor of Coronado.

On March 27, 1942, the War Powers Act was passed giving the government the power of possession. In May the Navy budgeted $13.5 million for construction of a hospital with storage and training facilities. In June condemnation proceedings were initiated to obtain title to over 113,000 acres of the Santa Margarita. Wartime needs rushed the Courts and on July 9, 1942, the Marine Corps was given immediate possession of the property. The purchase price approved by the Federal Courts in San Diego on April 12, 1943, was $4.1 million for 121,387 acres.

Before the first combat-destined troops arrived in August of 1942, the construction budget was increased by $13.6 million to provide for a 20,000-Marine training facility. In current times the Base population ranges from 35,000 to 40,000. Marine staffing varies from 28,000 to 32,000, plus 4000 to 5000 dependents and about 3000 civilian workers. The Base payroll is estimated to be $280 million a year. Civilian agriculture of Base land is said to earn about $350,000 annually for the U.S. Government.

A fascinating book is *Rancho Santa Margarita Remembered* by Jerome W. Baumgartner whose father lived on the Ranch for many years. The ISBN number is 0-931832-23-3. The story of Camp Pendleton is well told in *Marines of the Margarita* by Witty and Morgan. The publisher is Frye & Smith, Ltd. of San Diego, California.

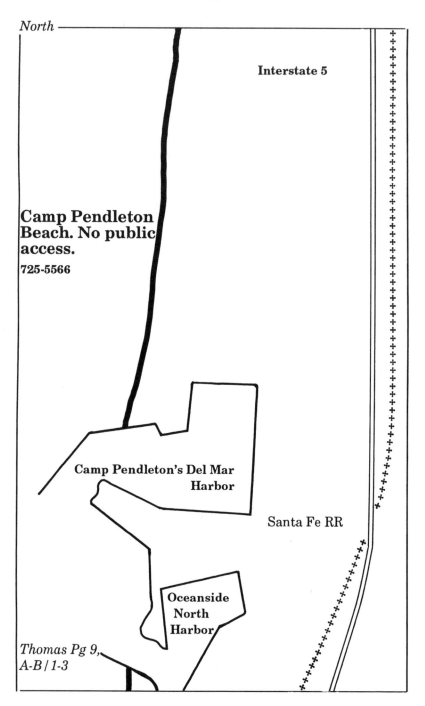

North

Interstate 5

Camp Pendleton Beach. No public access.

725-5566

Camp Pendleton's Del Mar Harbor

Santa Fe RR

Oceanside North Harbor

Thomas Pg 9, A-B / 1-3

Beach Walking in San Diego County

Thomas Guide Pg 9, A-B / 1-3   **Camp Pendleton Beach
Oceanside North Harbor**

Except for the area identified as Oceanside North Harbor (*Pg 9,
B / 4*), this beach and land is a portion of the Camp Pendleton
military reservation. Public access is not permitted.

Highway bridges over the tidelands flat two-miles north of
Oceanside span the Pacific outfall of the Santa Margarita River.

To reach Oceanside's North Harbor take Harbor Drive (*Pg 9,
B / 4*) off Interstate 5 and merge left under the overpass. Remain
left over the RR and turn left at the end of Harbor Drive.
Quickly turn right as you enter the Oceanside Harbor complex
and follow direction signs to 'North Harbor' and the 'Villa
Marina Hotel'. There is no beach or swimming in this section of
the harbor. An excellent walkway borders the marina. It is
1.2ml long from the harbor entrance to the hotel. There are
restrooms, showers, fountains, benches, BBQs and picnic tables.

A child's playground and fishing pier are located in this area.
Metered street parking and car lots are plentiful. Public
telephones are available and the Harbor Police office is centrally
located. The information telephone number is 966-4570. Public
transportation is via NCTD #312: Schedules from 722-6283.

Beach Walking in San Diego County

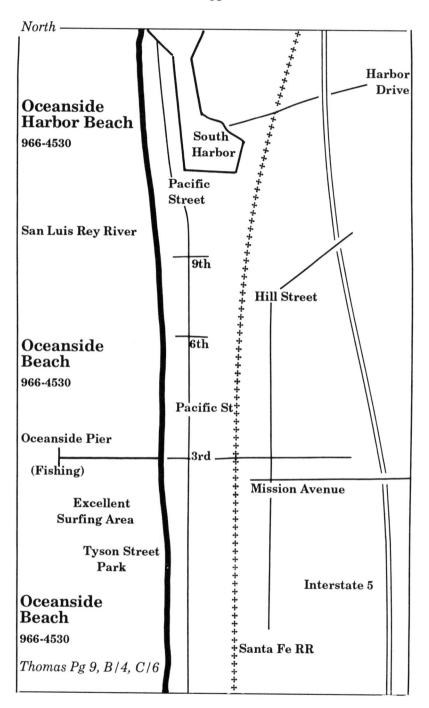

Harbor Drive

Oceanside Harbor Beach

966-4530

South Harbor

Pacific Street

San Luis Rey River

9th

Hill Street

Oceanside Beach

966-4530

6th

Pacific St

Oceanside Pier

(Fishing)

3rd

Mission Avenue

Excellent Surfing Area

Tyson Street Park

Interstate 5

Oceanside Beach

966-4530

Thomas Pg 9, B/4, C/6

Santa Fe RR

Beach Walking in San Diego County

Thomas Guide Pg 9, B/4, C/6   **Oceanside Beaches**

To enter the South Harbor area take Harbor Drive off Interstate 5 (*Pg 9, B/4*) and merge left under the overpass. Remain left over the RR and turn left at the end of Harbor Drive. As you enter the marina veer left for South Harbor and metered carlots.

It is .6ml from the entry drive to the South Harbor Beach (*Pg 9, B/5*) behind the Marina del Mar Hotel. There are carlots (Fee), restrooms, fire ring's, guard towers (Dial 911) and metered street parking. There are several food services. Public transport is by NCTD #312: Schedules from 722-6283.

9th, 6th and 3rd Streets are signed on Pacific Street for beach access. Streetside parking is metered. 3rd Street is open to vehicles down to The Strand (*Pg 9, B/5*) which leads one-way north to Ninth Street or one-way south to Wisconsin Avenue.

Oceanside's 3.7ml of beaches are always open. Restrooms are plentiful and each has showers and running water. Lifeguards monitor normal swimming hours (Dial 911) and there is a beach Police patrol. There are picnic tables, BBQs, fire rings, some shade and public telephones. Beach information from 966-4530.

Mission Avenue (*Pg 9, C/5*), off Interstate 5, leads toward the beach area. As you near the ocean, turn right on Hill Street one block to 3rd Street. Turn left on 3rd. At Pacific (*Pg 9, C/6*) go left or right for its many access ways to the beach. Street and lot parking is controlled and metered in this area. Or continue direct ahead to The Strand at beach level which is a one-way street north or south from the 3rd Street entry to the fishing pier. There is a children's playground in Tyson park (*Pg 9, C/6*), restrooms and limited handicapped parking off The Strand. Numerous food services are in the immediate pier area as is a most unique museum dedicated to the sport of surfing.

Surfing is best at Harbor Beach (*Pg 9, B/5*) and considered excellent in the Oceanside Fishing Pier area. All beaches are open for swimming. It is possible to walk the sand south to where the beach narrows at Eaton Street (*Pg 13, E/3*). There is beach access off Pacific Street, south of Wisconsin Avenue (*Pg 13, C/1*) down to Morse Way at Buccaneer Beach. (*Pg 13, D/2*)

Beach Walking in San Diego County

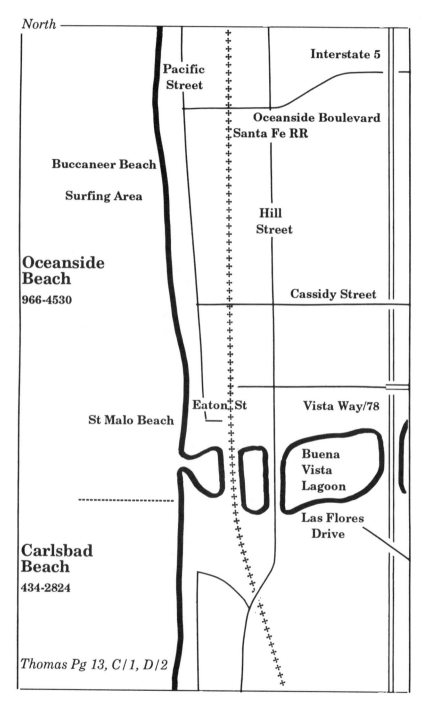

North

Pacific
Street

Interstate 5

Oceanside Boulevard

Santa Fe RR

Buccaneer Beach

Surfing Area

Hill
Street

**Oceanside
Beach**
966-4530

Cassidy Street

St Malo Beach

Eaton St

Vista Way/78

Buena
Vista
Lagoon

Las Flores
Drive

**Carlsbad
Beach**
434-2824

Thomas Pg 13, C/1, D/2

Beach Walking in San Diego County

Thomas Guide Pg 13, C/1, D/2   # Oceanside Beaches
Carlsbad City Beach

Oceanside Boulevard, off Interstate 5 (*Pg 13, D/1*) is a direct route to Pacific Street and central areas of Oceanside Beaches.

Beach access off Pacific Street is possible between Wisconsin Ave and Morse Way at Buccaneer Beach. (*Pg 13, D/2*)

Buccaneer Beach, at 1506 South Pacific (*Pg 13, D/2*), has a carlot, restrooms, showers and snack bar. Public transportation is via NCTD #312: Schedules from 722-6283. Picnic tables, BBQs, shade and a public telephone are in an adjoining park. Oceanside sand beaches, open 24-hours, are patrolled by police and there is a lifeguard station at Buccaneer. The emergency lifeguard service number is 911.

South of Buccaneer, the only access to Oceanside Beach is a walkway next to 1639 Pacific Street and from the Buena Vista Lagoon outlet (*Pg 13, E/3*). This sand beach strip is of varying width. Surfing is reported to be excellent and walking north toward Oceanside Pier is easy. Scarce parking on Pacific Street.

Cassidy Street, off Interstate 5 (*Pg 13, E/2*), is a direct route to Pacific Street and the southern portion of Oceanside beaches.

Vista Way/78 (*Pg 13, E/2*) is not a direct route to the beach.

Eaton Street, at the South end of Pacific, fronts the gated residential area of St Malo and its private beach. However, all beach below the high-tide line is public and it is possible to walk the narrow St Malo sand strip to the end of Oceanside Beach.

Las Flores Drive (*Pg 13, F/3*) is not a route to the beach area.

Carlsbad City Beach begins at Buena Vista Lagoon (*Pg 13, E/3*) where there is a modest area of sand. South of Buena Vista the seashore is a narrow sand beach more suitable for surfing than swimming or walking. There are no facilities at this north end of the short strip of Carlsbad City Beach. Open 0600 to 2300.

Beach Walking in San Diego County

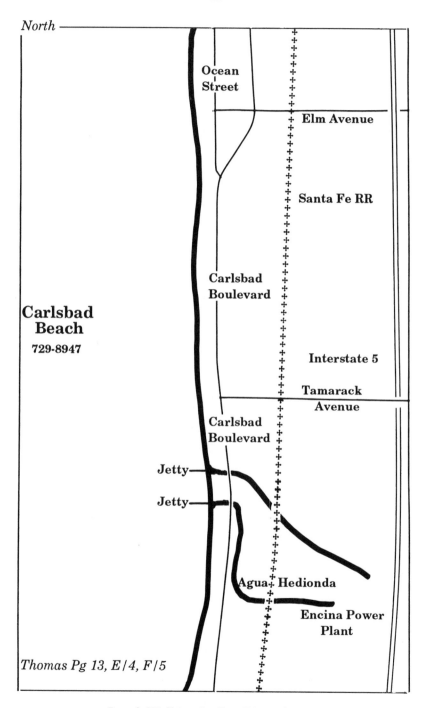

North

Ocean
Street

Elm Avenue

Santa Fe RR

Carlsbad
Boulevard

Carlsbad
Beach
729-8947

Interstate 5

Tamarack
Avenue

Carlsbad
Boulevard

Jetty

Jetty

Agua Hedionda

Encina Power
Plant

Thomas Pg 13, E/4, F/5

Beach Walking in San Diego County

Thomas Guide, Pg 13, E/4, F/5   **Carlsbad Beach**

Carlsbad's Ocean Street *(Pg 13, E/4)* has three points of sand beach access: From Christiansen Way (Showers), Grand Avenue and Carlsbad Village Drive *(Pg 13, F/4)* also known as Elm Avenue. In this area public transportation is available on Carlsbad Boulevard via NCTD #301: Schedules from 722-6283.

South of Elm Avenue there is ramp and stair sand beach access off Carlsbad Boulevard *(Pg 13, E/4)* down to Chinquapin Avenue *(Pg 13, F/5)*. Along this same stretch there is a fine bluff-top sidewalk overlooking a long walkable breakwater.

This 1.4ml section of Carlsbad Beach is sand with restrooms, showers, lifeguard towers and street parking between Pine and Tamarack *(Pg 13, F/5)* where there is a a beach-front carlot. There are a few fire rings for family picnics. This strip of beach (Open 0600-2300) is suitable for walking in all directions.

Two jetties limit beach walking but a pedestrian sidewalk on the Carlsbad Boulevard bridge *(Pg 13, F/6)* provides safe crossover.

Agua Hedionda Lagoon *(Pg 14, B/6)* includes the Encina Public Fishing area (Permit required) accessed from Carlsbad Blvd.

There is a sand bar ('Warm Water Beach') and lifeguard station (Dial 911) on Carlsbad Boulevard near the Encina Power plant.

Carlsbad State Beach *(Pg 19, A/1)*, which is 7429-feet long south of Cerezo Drive, is a sand/pebble beach. There is limited random access in this area and walking is best at low tide. At high tide some strips are blocked. Surfing is reported to be good.

Beach Walking in San Diego County

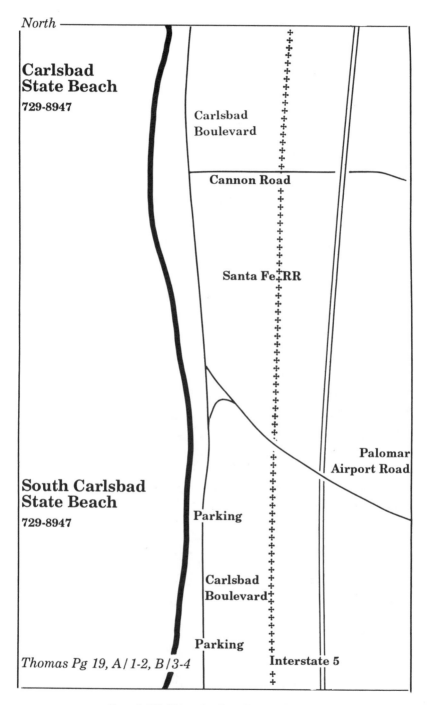

Beach Walking in San Diego County

Thomas Guide Pg 19,
A/1-2, B/3-4

Carlsbad State Beach
South Carlsbad State Beach

Use Cannon Road (*Pg 19, A/1*) off Interstate 15, drive west to
Carlsbad Boulevard and turn north or south. There is no beach
access north of Cannon Road until you reach the Agua Hedionda
Lagoon area. The first beach access south of Cannon Road is
near Palomar Airport Road (*Pg 19, B/2*).

Palomar Airport Road, off Interstate 5 (*Pg 19, B/2*), is a direct
route to Carlsbad Boulevard and this area of coastal beaches. An
unstable bluff area is fenced between Cerezo Drive and Palomar
Airport Road where there is streetside parking. A steep path
leads down to a surfer's cove about evenly divided between a
width of sand beach and narrow pebble beach. Both are walkable. There is no lifeguard station (Dial 911) here. Public
transportation is via NCTD #301 and #361. Schedules:722-6283.

This Carlsbad Boulevard parking lot is open from 0600 to 2300
daily. The pebble beach below is narrow and best for surfing.

This Carlsbad Boulevard parking lot is open from 0600 to 2300
daily. The pebble beach below is narrow and best for surfing.

Beach Walking in San Diego County

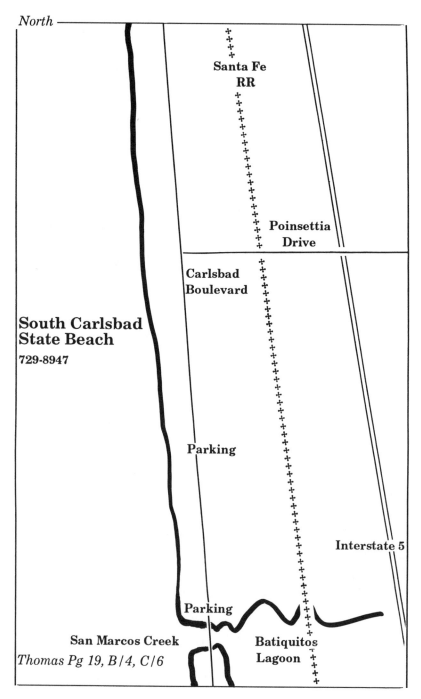

Thomas Pg 19, B/4, C/5 **South Carlsbad State Beach**

This entire stretch of narrow pebble beach south to Batiquitos Lagoon (*Pg 19, D-E/6*) is where surfing is the favorite sport with swimming limited to specified areas. All Carlsbad State Beaches are open from 0600 to 2300. Public transportation on Carlsbad Blvd. is via NCTD #301 and #361. Schedules from 722-6283.

Use Poinsettia Drive (*Pg 19, C/4*) off Interstate 5 to reach this area. California's South Carlsbad State Beach Campground, with 3.4ml of beach, is at the end of Poinsettia Drive but can only be entered off Carlsbad Boulevard. Reservations (729-8947) are advised. The campground has eight exits onto the narrow pebble beach which has lifeguard towers (Dial 911). Beachwalking is difficult because of the pebble shore. There is very limited visitor parking. In the campground there are restrooms, showers, tables, fire rings, shade and a food store. There is a north/south path along Carlsbad Boulevard.

This Carlsbad Boulevard parking lot (*Pg 19, C/5*) is open from 0600 to 2300 daily. The narrow pebble beach is used for surfing.

This Carlsbad Boulevard parking lot (*Pg 19, C/6*) is open from 0600 to2300 daily. The pebble beach is wide, has a lifeguard station and is best used for surfing. Walking is difficult.

Beach Walking in San Diego County

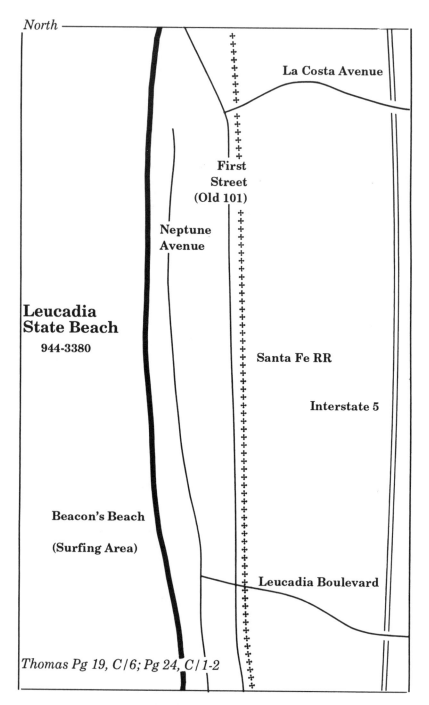

North ──────

La Costa Avenue

First
Street
(Old 101)

Neptune
Avenue

**Leucadia
State Beach**

944-3380

Santa Fe RR

Interstate 5

Beacon's Beach

(Surfing Area)

Leucadia Boulevard

Thomas Pg 19, C/6; Pg 24, C/1-2

Beach Walking in San Diego County

Thomas Guide   **Leucadia State Beach**
Pg 19, C/6; Pg 24, C/1-2   **Beacon's Beach**

La Costa Avenue (*Pg 19, D/6*) leads to First Street (Old 101)
from Interstate 5 but does not provide direct beach access.
Public transportation on First Street is via NCTD #301 and
#361: Schedules from 722-6283.

Grandview Beach (*Pg 24, C/1*) is at the end of Grandview
Avenue off First Street. Drive to Neptune Avenue, turn right
one block to a City of Encinitas Parking lot (Open 0600-2200)
and the beach access stairway at Sea Bluffe.

Leucadia State Beach (*Pg 19, C/2*) was once known as Ponto
State Beach. It is a very narrow 1.4ml pebble beach better ap-
preciated for surfing than for swimming. There are no facilities.
Low-tide beach walking is possible. For lifeguards Dial 911.

Beacon's Beach is reached by using the Leucadia Boulevard exit
(*Pg 24, D/2*) off Interstate 5. Leucadia ends at Neptune Avenue.
Turn right to 984 Neptune at Diana Street. Beacon's Beach (*Pg
24, C/2*) has a carlot open from 0600 to 2200, public telephone,
and steps to the pebble beach. No other facilities. There is no
other beach access from Neptune except at Sea Bluffe (*Pg 24,
C/1*). Controlled streetside parking is very scarce.

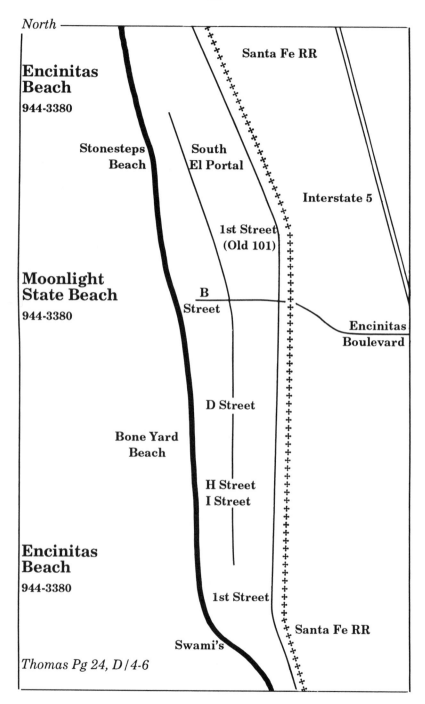

North

Encinitas
Beach
944-3380

Santa Fe RR

Stonesteps
Beach

South
El Portal

Interstate 5

1st Street
(Old 101)

Moonlight
State Beach
944-3380

B
Street

Encinitas
Boulevard

D Street

Bone Yard
Beach

H Street
I Street

Encinitas
Beach
944-3380

1st Street

Swami's

Santa Fe RR

Thomas Pg 24, D/4-6

Beach Walking in San Diego County

Encinitas Beach
Moonlight State Beach

Stonesteps Beach, near Seaside Gardens (*Pg 24, C/4*), is reached via South El Portal Street off 1st Street. Street parking is limited. There is a narrow sand beach (Open 0400-0200), lifeguard service (Dial 911) and excellent swimming. Beach walking is possible north and south at low tide. Public transit on 1st Street is via NCTD #301, #361. Schedules from 722-6283.

Moonlight Beach (*Pg 24, D/4*) is entered from Encinitas Boulevard, off Interstate 5 (*Pg 24, E/4*). There are car parks on C Street and 3rd Street. At Moonlight there are restooms, public telephones, a snack bar, running water, showers, fire rings and picnic tables. The one-third mile sand beach (Open 0400-0200) has a lifeguard station (Dial 911) and can be walked north and south. Family swimming is popular at this fine beach.

There are pebble beach access stairs on D Street at 4th Street. H Street has a viewpoint and picnic tables. No beach access. Boneyard Beach is between E and J Streets. No facilities. I Street has a viewpoint and picnic tables. No beach access.

Swami's, the pebble beach below Sea Cliff County Park (*Pg 24, D/6*), has a carlot (Open 0500-2200) at 1298 1st Street (Old 101), one block south of K Street. There are restrooms, tables, BBQs and public telephones in the bluff-top park. Stairs lead down to the narrow pebble beach world-renowned for surfing. Lifeguard tower (Dial911). Little beach-walking is possible.

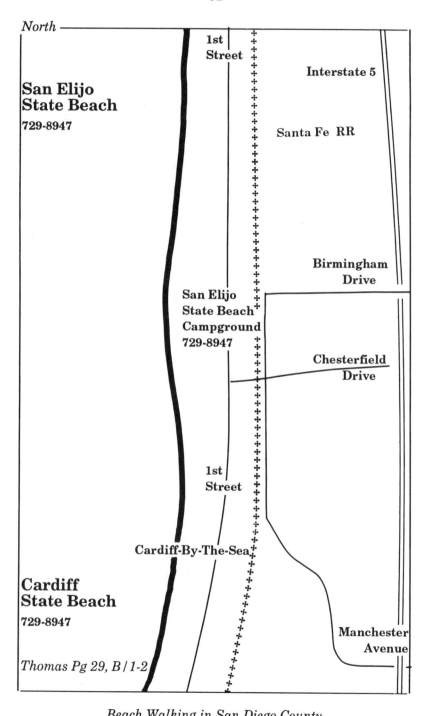

North

San Elijo State Beach

729-8947

1st Street

Interstate 5

Santa Fe RR

Birmingham Drive

San Elijo State Beach Campground 729-8947

Chesterfield Drive

1st Street

Cardiff-By-The-Sea

Cardiff State Beach

729-8947

Manchester Avenue

Thomas Pg 29, B / 1-2

Beach Walking in San Diego County

Thomas Guide Pg 29, B/1-2   **San Elijo State Beach
                                      Cardiff State Beach**

Streetside parking on 1st Street is possible from 0500 to 2400, south from Swami's to near San Elijo State Campground. A rocky waterfront inhibits shore walks between the sites.

Most of the 1.7ml San Elijo State Beach (*Pg 29, B/2*) is a narrow pebble shore more suitable for surfing than walking or swimming. There is a 2.5 mile walking and bike path along 1st Street from San Elijo Lagoon, northward to Swami's in Encinitas.

Public transit on 1st Street to Birmingham Drive is via NCTD # 301 and #361. South of Birmingham it is NCTD # 301 and #308.

San Elijo State Beach Campground (*Pg 29, C/2*) is reached via Birmingham Drive, off Interstate 5 (*Pg 29, B/1*). Turn left at the end of Birmingham to Chesterfield, then right across the railroad tracks and right again on 1st. Go two blocks to the entry. The campground has restrooms, showers, running water and assigned camp sites. Stairs lead to the pebble beach, known as Cardiff Pipes. Lifeguard stations (Dial 911). A 1st Street path leads north to Swami's and south to San Elijo Lagoon.

Manchester Avenue (*Pg 29, C/2*), off Interstate 5, provides indirect access to this beach area. At Chesterfield turn left over the railroad tracks then left on 1st Street to reach the site.

There are several quality restaurants in this beach-front area.

Cardiff Seaside Park (*Pg 29, B/3*) has a carlot, restrooms and running water. The beach, known as Cardiff Reef, has both sand and pebble areas. It narrows to the north and has a rock seawall and sand beach on the south known as George's/Cardiff.

Beach Walking in San Diego County

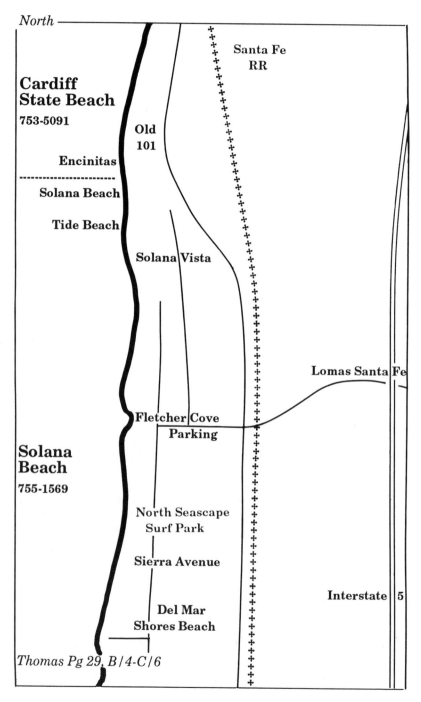

Beach Walking in San Diego County

Thomas Guide Pg 29, B/4-C/6 **Cardiff State Beach**
Solana Beach

To reach Cardiff State Beach use Lomas Santa Fe Drive *(Pg 29, C/4)* off Interstate 5. At 1st Street (Old 101) turn right and continue one mile to the pebble beach *(Pg 29, B/3)*. A carlot is open 0700-2300. There are restrooms, showers and guard towers (Dial 911). Public transit by NCTD # 309, # 361. Schedules: 722-6283.

Tide Beach *(Pg 29, B/4)* is reached via Lomas Santa Fe Drive *(Pg 29, C/4)* off Interstate 5. Drive west past 1st Street (Old 101) to Acacia Avenue. Turn right to Solana Vista Drive on the left. It leads to Tide Beach access stairs *(Pg 29, B/4)*. Street parking is limited. There is a lifeguard tower (Dial 911) and a pleasant sand beach (Open 0600-2200) which is walkable north and south. There are no other facilities at this swimmers site.

Fletcher Cove *(Pg 29, B/5)*, also known as 'Pill Box', is at the end of Lomas Santa Fe Drive. The beach and carlot at Plaza Street and South Sierra Avenue are open from 0600 to 2200. There are restrooms, showers, telephones and fire rings. The Solana Beach Marine Safety department (755-1569) is headquartered here. For life-guard emergencies Dial 911. Sand beach walking is excellent north and south. For tide/weather: 755-2971. Public transit by NCTD # 301, # 308. Schedules: 722-6283.

To reach Del Mar Shores and North Seascape use Lomas Santa Fe *(Pg 29, C/4)* off Interstate 5. Drive west past 1st Street and turn left on Sierra Avenue for southern Solana Beach.

North Seascape *(Pg 29, B/5)* has an access walkway with parking adjacent to 353 Sierra Avenue. It is a sand beach, walkable north/south, with a guard tower (Dial 911) but no facilities.

Del Mar Shores *(Pg 29. C/6)* has public parking at the corner of Sierra Avenue and Del Mar Shores Terrace. Public access is at the west end of Terrace. It is a sand beach with a guard tower (Dial 911) but no facilities. It is walkable north/south.

Beach Walking in San Diego County

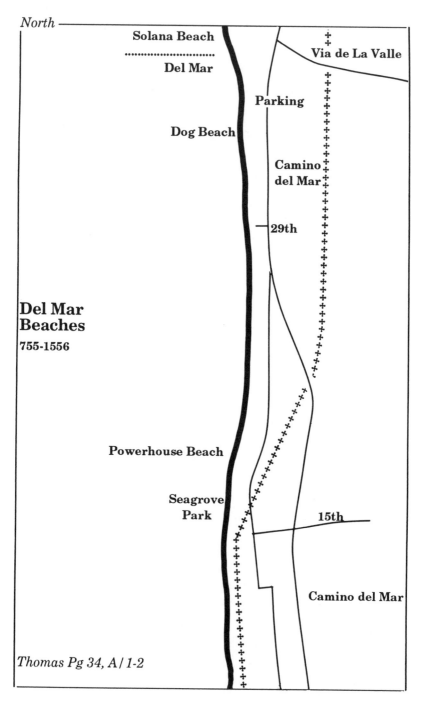

North

Solana Beach

Del Mar

Via de La Valle

Parking

Dog Beach

Camino
del Mar

29th

Del Mar
Beaches

755-1556

Powerhouse Beach

Seagrove
Park

15th

Camino del Mar

Thomas Pg 34, A / 1-2

Beach Walking in San Diego County

Thomas Guide Pg 34, A/1-2   # Del Mar Beaches

Use Via de La Valle (*Pg 29, C/6*) off Interstate 5, west to
Camino del Mar. Turn right for Solana Beach, left for Del Mar
beaches. Public transit via NCTD #301. Schedules: 722-6283.

'Dog Beach' (*Pg 29, C/6*), so called because dogs are allowed to
run freely, is a wide sand beach with guard towers (Dial 911)
and excellent walking potential in both directions. There is roadside parking between Via de La Valle and the San Dieguito
River (*Pg 34, A/1*) where the beach area is called 'Rivermouth'.

There is beach access at the end of all streets from 29th Street
(*Pg 34. A/1*) southward to 15th Street. However street parking
is severely limited and controls are enforced.

Del Mar Beaches are open 24 hours daily. The central lifeguard
tower (755-1556) is staffed from 0900 to 2000 with additional
towers operational as beach use demands. There are no fire
rings or picnic tables. Use of portable cookers is permitted on the
sand with cleanup mandatory. For an emergency Dial 911.

Seagrove Park (*Pg 34, A/2*) is located at the corner of 15th
Street and Coast Boulevard. There is a children's playground,
picnic tables and benches but no other facilities. There is
metered underground parking off 15th between Coast and
Camino del Mar. Streetside parking is severely limited and controls are enforced. There are many fine restaurants in the area.

Southward there is no beach access off Ocean Ave. (*Pg 34, A/3*)
until 13th Street, from which it is possible to reach narrow sand.

Beach Walking in San Diego County

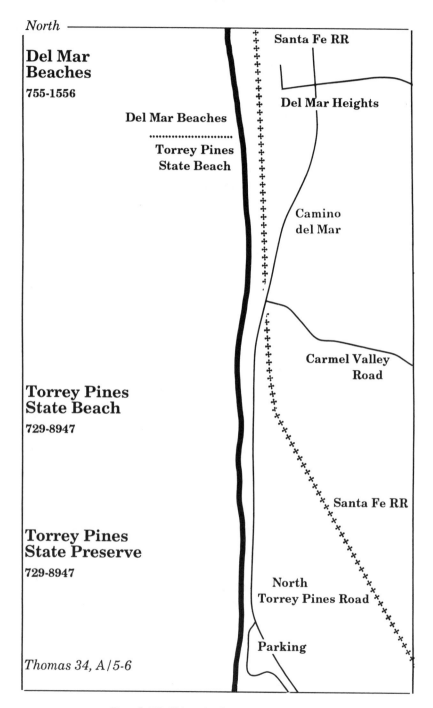

Del Mar Beaches

755-1556

Santa Fe RR

Del Mar Heights

Del Mar Beaches

Torrey Pines State Beach

Camino del Mar

Torrey Pines State Beach

729-8947

Carmel Valley Road

Torrey Pines State Preserve

729-8947

Santa Fe RR

North Torrey Pines Road

Thomas 34, A/5-6

Parking

Beach Walking in San Diego County

Thomas Guide, Pg 34, A/5-6   **Del Mar Beaches**
Torrey Pines State Beach

To reach Del Mar's southern beaches *(Pg 34, A/4)* take Del Mar
Heights Road *(Pg 34. A-B/4)* off Interstate 5. Cross Camino del
Mar onto 4th Street and turn right on Stratford Court. There is
random access at the end of all streets from 4th to 13th but
scarce streetside parking. Beach access involves scrambling
down a shallow bluff and crossing the Santa Fe RR tracks to a
narrow sand beach. There are no facilities in this area. There is
a dangerous 1.5ml walking path beside the tracks from the Del
Mar RR station south to Carmel Valley Road (*Pg 34, A/5)* .

To reach the 4.4-mile Torrey Pines State Beach *(Pg 34, A/5)*
take Carmel Valley Road off Interstate 5. Turn left for Torrey
Pines State Beach. There is some roadside parking on the west
side of Camino del Mar but only difficult bluff paths leading to
the narrow sand beach below. There is a walking path along
Camino del Mar which leads to Encinitas and beyond. An excellent carlot (Entry fee) with restrooms, beach access and public
telephones is at the west end of McGonigle Road (*Pg 34, A/5)*.

This area of Torrey Pines State Beach *(Pg 34, A/5-6)* has roadside parking on the ocean side of North Torrey Pines Road.
Public transit is by NCTD # 301. Schedules: 722-6283.

The entrance (Fee) to Torrey Pines State Preserve *(Pg 34, A/6)*
leads to the 1750-acre park. Near the kiosk are restrooms,
showers, carlot, telephones, picnic tables and lifeguard tower
(Dial 911) for the sand beach. The winding road into the
Preserve is route of the mid-20s main road from San Diego to
Los Angeles. Some original sections are only 16-feet wide.

Beach Walking in San Diego County

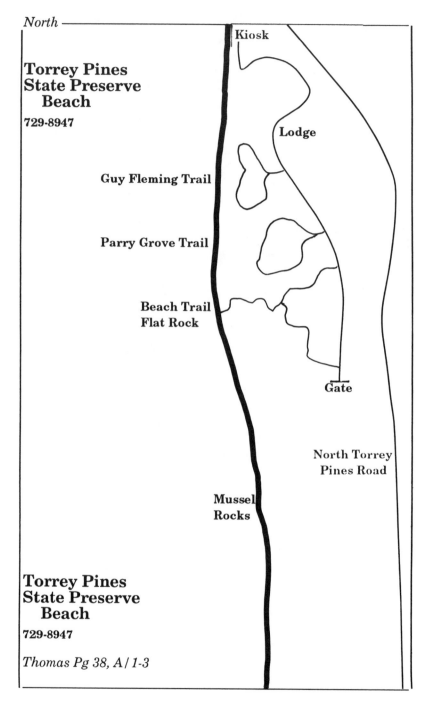

North ———

**Torrey Pines
State Preserve
Beach**

729-8947

Kiosk

Lodge

Guy Fleming Trail

Parry Grove Trail

**Beach Trail
Flat Rock**

Gate

**North Torrey
Pines Road**

**Mussel
Rocks**

**Torrey Pines
State Preserve
Beach**

729-8947

Thomas Pg 38, A / 1-3

Beach Walking in San Diego County

Torrey Pines State Preserve

To enter the Torrey Pines State Preserve take Carmel Valley
Road off Interstate 5. Drive West and at Camino del Mar/North
Torrey Pines Road (*Pg 34, A/5*) turn left. At one mile you will
find the Preserve entry gate (Fee) with its parking lot,
restrooms, showers, running water and public telephone. There
is access to a wide sand beach with a lifeguard tower (Dial 911)
at this point. The Preserve is open from 0900 to sunset. Acces-
sible State beaches are open from 0800 to sunset.

Follow direction signs to the Torrey Pines State Preserve (*Pg 38,
A/2*), a 1750-acre natural site with well maintained trails. Only
one, the Beach Trail, leads down to Torrey Pines State Beach.
Portions of the trail are steep and narrow. Other trails are loop
walks or lead to observation points of exceptional interest.

The Lodge and Preserve Headquarters have parking lots,
restrooms, public telephone, museum and a book store. There is
another restroom in a second parking area a short distance from
the headquarters. Here, a wall map of trails defines their level
of difficulty and should be consulted by first-time visitors.
There is no public transportation into the Preserve area.

A unique feature of the Torrey Pines State Beach is an underwater park which is protected and maintained for marine
research and enjoyment by scuba and snorkel divers.
The narrow sand beach is protected by lifeguard towers and
suitable for north/south walks. Picnicing is permitted on the
beach but nowhere else in the Preserve. Flat Rock is unique for
its rectangular tidal basin and spectacular breaking waves.

The State Parks system looks upon the Torrey Pines Preserve
(*Pg 38, A/1-2*) as an island of wilderness in an urban environ-
ment. The nation's rarest pine tree (*Pinius Torreyana*) grows
only here and on Santa Rosa Island.

Those portions of the area south of the locked gate are occupied
by a San Diego City golf course, Scripps Hospital and Scripps
Research Center)*Pg 38, B/4*). Beach access is not possible from
their properties. (*Pg 38, B/3-4*).

Beach Walking in San Diego County

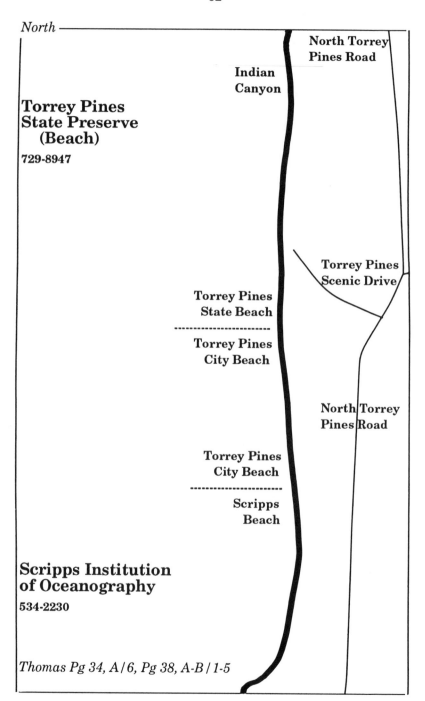

North Torrey
Pines Road

Indian
Canyon

**Torrey Pines
State Preserve
(Beach)**
729-8947

Torrey Pines
Scenic Drive

Torrey Pines
State Beach

Torrey Pines
City Beach

North Torrey
Pines Road

Torrey Pines
City Beach

Scripps
Beach

**Scripps Institution
of Oceanography**
534-2230

Thomas Pg 34, A / 6, Pg 38, A-B / 1-5

Beach Walking in San Diego County

Thomas Guide
Pg 34, A/6, Pg 38, A-B/1-5

Torrey Pines State Beach
Torrey Pines City Beach
Scripps Beach

To reach this area take Genesee Avenue (*Pg 38, C/5*) off Interstate 5. Drive west toward the ocean and where Genesee and North Torrey Pines meet (*Pg 38, B/5*) veer left ahead onto North Torrey Pines Road.

On the right look for poorly marked Torrey Pines Scenic Drive (*Pg 38, B/5*) with a 'Gliderport' sign. Turn right to Gliderport parking lots. Public transit by SDT # 34, Schedules: 233-3004.

There are two 'Black's Beaches' in this area. At the bottom of the wandering beach access path turn right to Torrey Pines State Beach (Black's Nude Beach) where nude bathing is countenanced. Turn left at the waterfront to Torrey Pines San Diego City Beach (mistakenly called Black's Beach) where nude bathing is not permitted. There are no facilities at either sand beach.

The Gliderport (*Pg 38, B/5*) is used for parasailing and hanggliding on rising air currents at the ocean-front bluff. A restaurant, hang-glider school and telephone are on the premises.

Scripps Institution of Oceanography (*Pg 44, A/2*) controls the sand beach south of the dotted line. There is no direct access to their beach in this area. Walkers reach Scripps Beach along the tide line from the Gliderport path to Torrey Pines City Beach.

Beach Walking in San Diego County

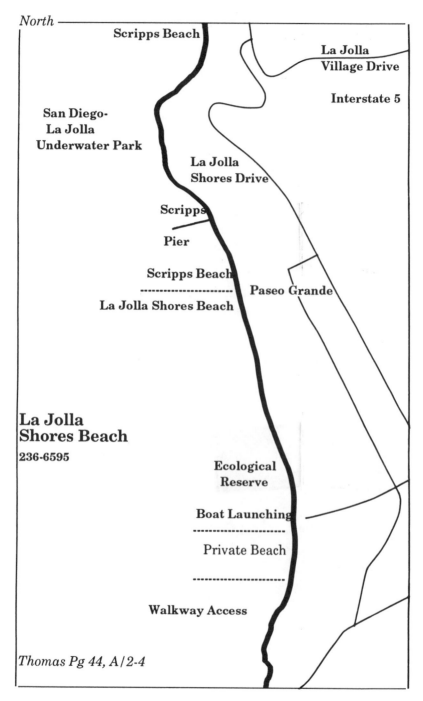

North

Scripps Beach

La Jolla
Village Drive

Interstate 5

San Diego-
La Jolla
Underwater Park

La Jolla
Shores Drive

Scripps

Pier

Scripps Beach

La Jolla Shores Beach

Paseo Grande

La Jolla
Shores Beach

236-6595

Ecological
Reserve

Boat Launching

Private Beach

Walkway Access

Thomas Pg 44, A/2-4

Beach Walking in San Diego County

Scripps Beach
La Jolla Shores Beach

Scripps Beach is reached off Interstate 5 via the La Jolla Village Drive exit (*Pg 44, C/2*). Drive west to North Torrey Pines Road. Turn right then quickly left onto La Jolla Shores Drive (*Pg 44, B/2*). Look for Paseo Grande (*Pg 44, A/3*) on the right as you pass Scripps Institution of Oceanography. At the corner of Paseo Grande and Discovery Street is a small parking lot with beach access steps. There is beach access from Scripps' campus north of the pier (*Pg 44, A/2*). Restrooms are in the Aquarium. Street parking is very limited and weekday parking on campus is by permit only. Public transit is via SDT # 34. Schedules: 233-3004.

Scripps' sand beach offers good surfing, guard towers and fine tidepools at the north end. It is possible to beach-walk 1.2ml south to La Jolla Shores Beach. This coastal area, The La Jolla Underwater Park, is a marine preserve for research and enjoyment of scuba divers and snorkel-equipped swimmers.

La Jolla Shores Beach (*Pg 44, A/3*) is reached off Paseo Grande. This large sand beach has restrooms, guard towers (Dial 911), a paved beachfront walkway and fire rings. Kellogg Park is adjacent with grassed areas, BBQs, picnic tables and some shade. There are numerous food services in the area. The large carlot is open from 0400 to 2200. Tide and weather information: 225-9492. Public transit: SDT # 34. Schedules from: 233-3004.

A boat launching ramp is entered off the end of Avenida de La Playa (*Pg 44, A/4*). This is the south limit of La Jolla Shores Beach. The adjoining private beach does not allow entry. A small public beach access walkway is located at the intersection of Spindrift Drive and Roseland Drive (*Pg 44, A/4*). Steps lead into breaking waves at high tide. Street parking is limited. This is off Torrey Pines Road via Princess Street (*Pg 43A, F/1*)

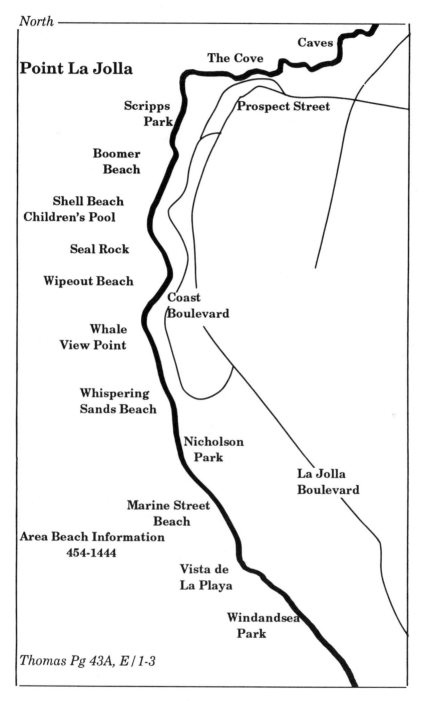

North

Point La Jolla

Caves

The Cove

Scripps
Park

Prospect Street

Boomer
Beach

Shell Beach
Children's Pool

Seal Rock

Wipeout Beach

Coast
Boulevard

Whale
View Point

Whispering
Sands Beach

Nicholson
Park

La Jolla
Boulevard

Marine Street
Beach

Area Beach Information
454-1444

Vista de
La Playa

Windandsea
Park

Thomas Pg 43A, E / 1-3

Beach Walking in San Diego County

La Jolla Beaches

To reach La Jolla's fine beaches from the North, leave Interstate 5 via the La Jolla Village Drive exit (*Pg 44, C/2*). Proceed west to Torrey Pines Road and turn left. Continue 2.75-miles ahead to Prospect Street (*Pg 43A, F/1*) and turn right. It is one long block to Coast Boulevard and its angled downhill right turn.

From the south, leave Interstate 5 via the Adarth Road exit (*Pg 44, B/5*). Follow Adarth over the hill to its merge with Torrey Pines Road. Public transit is via SDT #34. Schedules: 233-3004.

Coast Boulevard (*Pg 43A, E/1*) provides access to a wide array of beach sites for surfing, swimming, sun-bathing or girl-watching. The Children's Pool is adjacent to a guard tower at Jenner Street. The grassed Ellen Scripps Park (*Pg 43A, E/1-2*) offers complete recreational facilities including picnic tables, BBQs, shade and guard towers (Dial 911). Restrooms, telephones and snack food are available. This is a popular tourist area. Parking is limited on Coast Boulevard and side streets. A bluff-side carlot is at Coast and Coast Blvd. South.

Beach walking is limited in this area as walkable sand beaches are small and separated by rock outcroppings which make coast passage almost impossible. The alternative is a network of paths in the Scripps Park and along the bluffs both north and south. Walkers and joggers make extensive use of La Jolla parks.

The Marine Street Beach (*Pg 43A, E/2*) is reached off La Jolla Boulevard via Marine Street or Sea Lane. Street parking is limited. There are no facilities. Beach walking is possible on about one mile of medium-wide sand beach.

Windandsea Park (Vista La Playa) (*Pg 43A, E/3*) is a sand beach along Neptune Place at Nautilus Street off La Jolla Boulevard. There is a small carlot and some shade on the beach. Beach walking is possible. There are no facilities. A surfing site.

La Jolla Strand Park (*Pg 43A, E/4*) is a narrow sand beach along Neptune Place at Gravilla Street off La Jolla Boulevard. Beach walking is possible north to Windandsea Park. There are no facilities at this site. Scarce side-street parking.

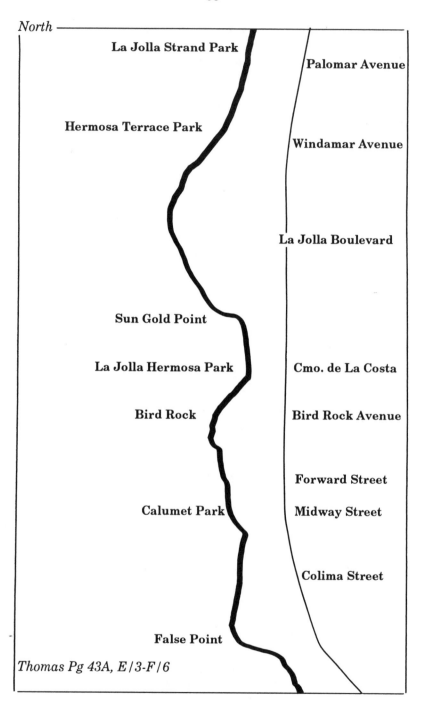

North

La Jolla Strand Park

Palomar Avenue

Hermosa Terrace Park

Windamar Avenue

La Jolla Boulevard

Sun Gold Point

La Jolla Hermosa Park

Cmo. de La Costa

Bird Rock

Bird Rock Avenue

Forward Street

Calumet Park

Midway Street

Colima Street

False Point

Thomas Pg 43A, E/3-F/6

Beach Walking in San Diego County

Thomas Guide Pg 43A, E/3-F-6   **La Jolla Beaches**

To reach other La Jolla's beaches from the north, leave Interstate 5 via La Jolla Village Drive exit (*Pg 44, C/2*). Proceed west to Torrey Pines Road and turn left. Continue 3.25-miles ahead to Girard Avenue (*Pg 43A, E/2*) and turn left. Make a quick right on Pearl and then go left on La Jolla Boulevard which is the seventh street. From the south, leave Interstate 5 via the Adarth Road exit (*Pg 44, B/5*). Follow Adarth over the hill to Torrey Pines Road. Public transit via SDT # 34. Schedules: 233-3004.

La Jolla Strand Park (*Pg 43A, E/4*) is off Neptune Place and Palomar Avenue. Street parking is very limited. Southward on Camino de La Costa (*Pg 43A, E/4*), beach access is next to a residence at 6060. Street parking is limited. No beach facilities.

Sun Gold Point (*Pg 43A, E/5*) has no beach. Rock scrambling is possible. Benches and shore stairs are at the end of La Canada.

La Jolla Hermosa Park (*Pg 43A, E/5*) on Chelsea Avenue does not offer beach access: Picnic tables, grass but no facilities.

Bird Rock (*Pg 43A, E/5*) is a nesting site for marine life. Stairs provide shoreline access from Bird Rock Avenue. The rocky beach is seldom walkable. Street parking is scarce. No facilities.

Forward Street ends at the coast but offers no shoreline access.

Calumet Park (*Pg 43A, E/5*) does not offer beach access. There is grass and benches. No other facilities are at this viewpoint.

False Point (*Pg 43A, F/6*) can be visited from stairs at the end of Linda Way off Sea Ridge. The narrow beach is all pebbles except for a little sand at the southern end of the cove. No facilities.

Beach Walking in San Diego County

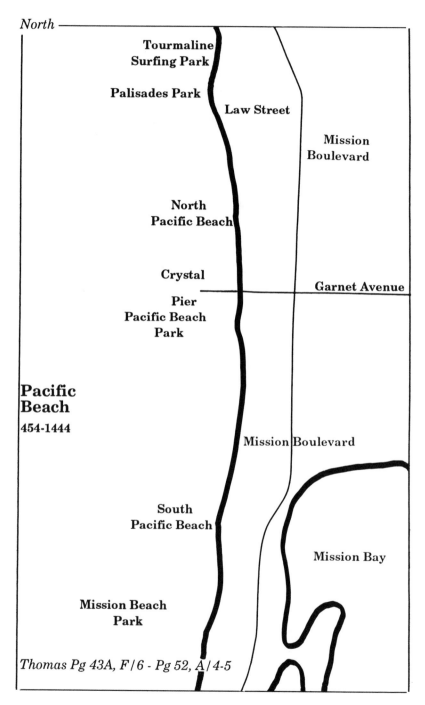

Pacific Beach

Pacific Beach is reached by following Garnet Avenue off Interstate 5 (*Pg 52, D/3*). Travel west to Mission Boulevard (*Pg 52, A/4*) and turn left or right on Mission as desired. Public transit via SDT # 9, # 27, # 30, # 81. Schedules: 233-3004.

Tourmaline Surfing Park (*Pg 43A, F/6*) is a medium-wide sand beach with restrooms, benches and parking lot. Swimming is not permitted at this surf beach. Beach-walking is possible one-half mile north, and about four miles south to the Mission Bay area.

Palisades Park (*Pg 52, A/3*) at the end of Law and Loring Streets is a bluff-top park with paved walkways, benches, fire rings, grass, restrooms and multiple viewpoints. There is access to the sand beach from this point. Street parking is limited.

North Pacific Beach (*Pg 52, A/4*) can be accessed from any street in its area. There are restrooms, fire rings and guard towers (Dial 911). There is a small carlot on Diamond Street.

Crystal Pier (*Pg 52, A/4*) supports a motel and provides public ocean fishing at the end of the pier. Restrooms, telephones and food services are in the area. Street parking is scarce. The adjacent wide sand beach has guard towers (Dial 911) and is a favorite surfing area. Fire rings are south of the Pier.

Pacific Beach Park (*Pg 52, A/4*) is a grassed park with a paved walkway separating the sand beach from land-side buildings.

South Pacific Beach (*Pg 52, A/5*) is a surfing area accessed from every East-West street. There are restrooms on Pacific Beach Boulevard at the ocean front (*Pg 52, A/5*) Fire rings, guard towers, snack services and wide sand make this a favorite area.

Mission Beach Park [Belmont Park] (*Pg 59, A/1-2*) is a popular sand beach for surfing. Other than a large car lot off Mission Boulevard (*Pg 52, A/1*), parking is scarce. Restrooms, showers, water and telephones are next to San Diego's roller coaster. Guard towers (Dial 911), picnic tables and fire rings are in the area. Public transit is via SDT # 34, # 81. Schedules: 233-3004.

Beach Walking in San Diego County

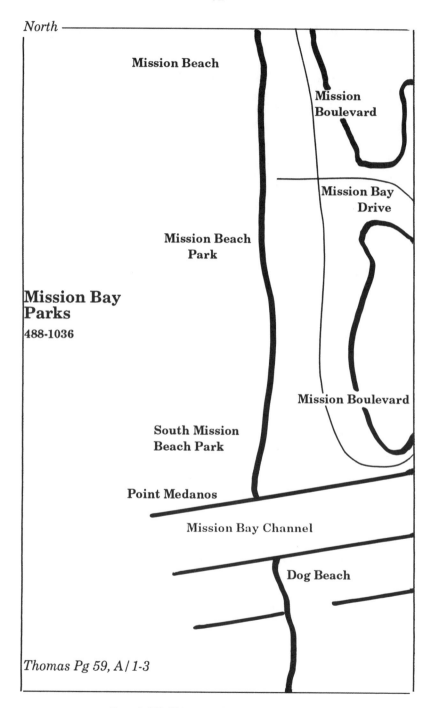

Beach Walking in San Diego County

Thomas Guide Pg 59, A/1-3   **Mission Beach
Mission Beach Park
Dog Beach**

Mission Beach is reached off Interstate 8. Exit onto Midway Drive. *(Pg 59, D/3)*. Turn right and watch right for a confusing loop turn *(Pg 59, C/2)* onto West Mission Bay Drive. Continue ahead on Mission Bay Drive to Mission Boulevard and go left or right. Also accessed from Garnet Avenue, Page 71. Public transit is via SDT # 34, # 81. Schedules from 233-3004.

Mission Beach *(Pg 52, A/5-6)* is a wide sand surfing/swimming beach with food services, paved ocean-front walk, fire rings, telephone and guard towers (Dial 911). Street parking is limited.

Mission Beach Park (Belmont Park) *(Pg 59, A/1)* has a large parking lot, restrooms, telephones, food services and guard towers. A grassed park area has picnic tables. Surfing is said to be excellent. The Belmont Roller Coaster is located here.

South Mission Beach Park *(Pg 59, A/2)* is the first of a variety of parks in the Mission Bay area. Access is from all streets but street parking is limited. There is a wide sand (surfing) beach with light and foghorn on the jetty. No public transportation.

Mission Bay Channel *(Pg 59, A-B/2)* is the entry point for thousands of small craft which live in the many Mission Bay marina's. The south jetty borders the San Diego River outfall.

Dog Beach, on which dogs may run loose, *(Pg 59, A/3)* is entered via Voltaire Street off West Point Loma Boulevard *(Pg 59, B-C/3)* in Ocean Beach. Careful footsteps are suggested. Public transit is via SDT # 35. Schedules: 233-3004. There are carlots, rest rooms, a guard tower (Dial 911) and fire rings. It is possible to beach-walk one mile south to the Ocean Beach Fishing Pier. A paved walkway borders the San Diego River channel.

Beach Walking in San Diego County

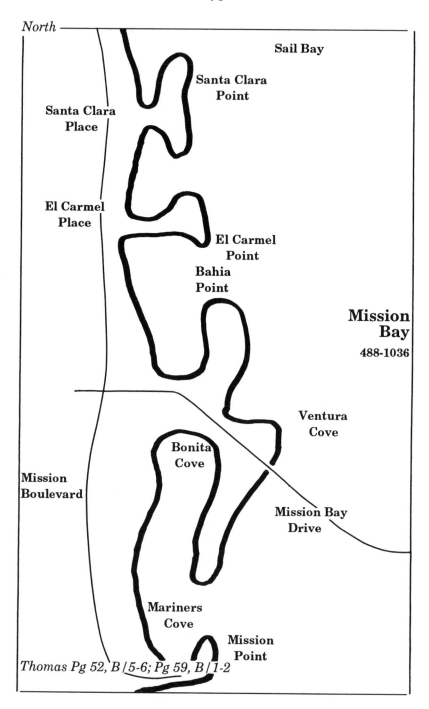

North ———

Sail Bay

Santa Clara
Point

Santa Clara
Place

El Carmel
Place

El Carmel
Point

Bahia
Point

**Mission
Bay**

488-1036

Ventura
Cove

Bonita
Cove

Mission
Boulevard

Mission Bay
Drive

Mariners
Cove

Mission
Point

Thomas Pg 52, B/5-6; Pg 59, B/1-2

Beach Walking in San Diego County

Mission Bay - West

Western shores of Mission Bay are best reached by following Interstate 8 West to the Midway exit *(Pg 59, D/3).* Turn right and watch right for a confusing loop return *(Pg 59, C/2)* leading to West Mission Bay Drive. Continue ahead to Mission Boulevard and turn left or right to the desired Mission Bay site. Public transit via SDT # 34, # 81. Schedules: 233-3004.

Santa Clara Point *(Pg 52, B/5)* is a San Diego City Recreation Center with a large carlot, restrooms, telephones, fire rings, picnic tables, grass parklands. totlot and a sailing school. Sand beaches have guard towers (Dial 911) and boat launch ramps.

El Carmel Point *(Pg 52, B/6)* is home to the Mission Bay Yacht Club. There is a carlot, sand beach, restrooms and guard towers. A marina is on the south. Public telephones and snack services.

Bahia Point *(Pg 59, B/1)* is a small public park at the rear of the Bahia Resort. There is a parking lot, fire rings, picnic tables, sand beach, restrooms, paved walkways and grassed picnic area on the bay. Public transit via SDT # 81. Schedules: 233-3004.

Ventura Cove *(Pg 59, B/1)* has a carlot, sand beach, walkways, grass, shade, picnic tables and guard tower (Dial 911).

Bonita Cove *(Pg 59, B/1)* is entered from Mission Bay Drive. There is a big parking lot, sand beach, totlot, fire rings, paved walkways and restrooms. Another entry is San Fernando Place *(Pg 59, A/1)* off Mission Boulevard. It leads to large parking lot, snack services, fire rings and access to Bonita Cove beaches. Public transit is via SDT # 81. Schedules from 233-3004.

Mariners Basin *(Pg 59, B/2)* has a broad sand beach but very limited parking. Use Bonita Cove parks and walk to Mariners. All beaches in the Mission Bay area are walkable. There is no public transportation to this Basin or Mission Point.

Mission Point *(Pg 59, B/2)* is a public park with paved walkways, carlot, restrooms, totlot, grass and picnic tables. There is no beach or water entry over rip rap channel banks.

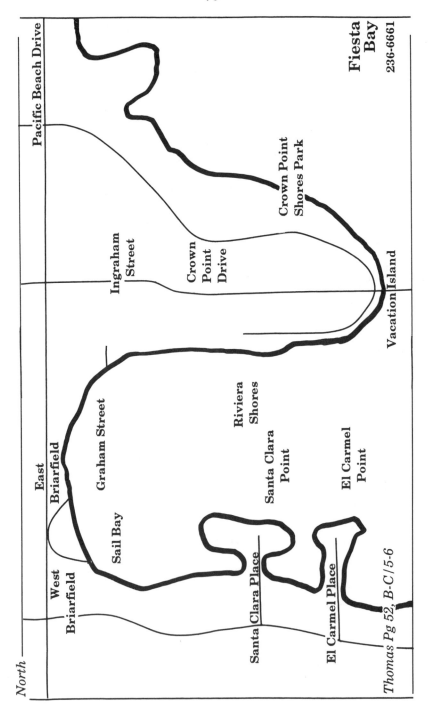

Beach Walking in San Diego County

Thomas Guide Pg 52, B-C/5-6

Sail Bay
Crown Point Shores
Mission Bay - North

For Mission Bay - North, use the Garnet Avenue exit from Interstate 5 (*Pg- 52, D/3*) and drive west to Ingraham Street. Turn left to Pacific Beach Drive (*Pg 52, B/4*) thence left or right to the beach. Transit via SDT # 34, # 81. Info: 233-3004.

West and East Briarfield (*Pg 52, B/5*) provide passage around private land from the west side of Sail Bay to the east side. There are benches along this popular sand beach area but no other facilities.

At the base of Faunel Street (*Pg 52, B/5*) is a nice grassed park with restrooms, showers, totlot, picnic tables and a guard tower (Dial 911). Car lot space is limited. There is access to paved and sand walkways in both directions around Sail Bay. There is a beach access walk at the end of Graham Street (*Pg 52, B/5*) but parking is scarce. There is no public transit to this area.

Riviera Shores' beach (*Pg 52, B/5*) narrows to the south. Street parking is very scarce in this area.

Riviera Drive (*Pg 59, B/5*) and Crown Point Drive (*Pg 52, C/5*) join at Ingraham and the Fisherman's Channel Bridge (*Pg 52, C/6*). Public transportation to this and the following area is via SDT # 9. Schedule information from 233-3004.

Crown Point Shores (*Pg 52, C/5*) is a large grassed park with shade and a car lot. There are several restrooms with showers, public telephones, fire rings, picnic tables, a sand beach and guard towers (Dial 911). This area is walkable north to the Least Tern Wildlife Refuge (*Pg 52, C/4*). South and north sections of the Park's waterfront are limited to swimming. The central section is for boat launching and water skiing.

To walk around private land and the Least Tern Wildlife Refuge north of Crown Point Shores, follow Olney Street (*Pg 52, C/4*) north to Grand Avenue. Walk east on Grand to the east side of Rose Creek (*Pg 52, D/4*). There is a narrow walkway leading south along the creek bank to De Anza Cove, Mission Bay beaches and walkways.

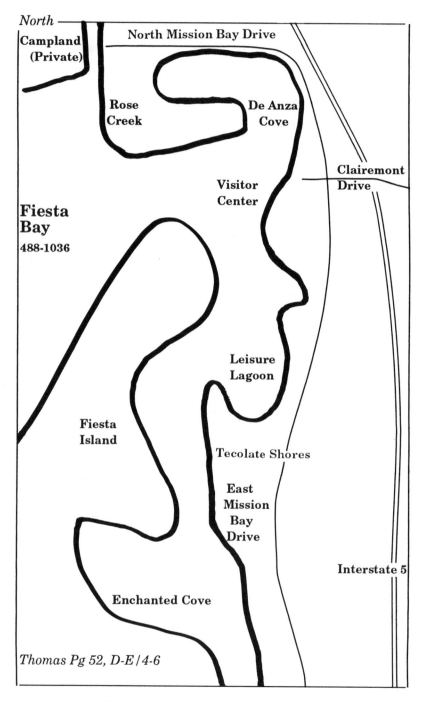

Beach Walking in San Diego County

Thomas Guide Pg 52, D-E/4-6   **Fiesta Bay**
                                       Visitor Center
                                     Mission Bay - East

This area is best entered from Clairemont Drive off Interstate 5
(*Pg 52, E/5*). Drive west toward the Bay and continue ahead
around the Visitor Center (*Pg 52, E/5*) to the carlot. The Visitor
Center is staffed by experts on local touring who provide maps
and information. There is a carlot, grass, shade, playground, totlot, telephones and restrooms. From there drive north or south
on Mission Bay Drive for waterfront access. There is no transit
service to this and the following areas.

On North Mission Bay Drive, next to the San Diego Boat & Ski
Club entrance (*Pg 52, D/4*), is a narrow walkway leading to
Grand Avenue along Rose Creek. Follow Grand west to Olney
Street, then south on Olney to Crown Point Shores (*Pg 52, C/5*).

De Anza Cove (*Pg 52, D/4*) has a car lot,, sand beach, boat
launching ramp, restrooms, grass, shade, fire rings, BBQs, picnic tables, totlot and guard towers (Dial 911). Paved and beach
walks lead southward. Campgrounds on the west are private.

Leisure Lagoon (*Pg 52, E/5*) has a sand beach, guard tower
(Dial 911), restrooms and paved walkways leading north to De
Anza Cove and south to Fiesta Island. Plus a carlot, grassed
parkland, totlot, fire rings, BBQs, picnic tables and shade trees.

Tecolate Shores Beach, south of Leisure Lagoon (*Pg 52, E/5*), is
grassed parkland with sand beach, BBQs, picnic tables, PAR
course, restrooms, playground, shade trees and guard tower
(Dial 911). The car lot fills early. Some limited street parking.

Fiesta Island (*Pg 52, D/6*) is a man-made recreational site
detailed on the following page. Entry is off Sea World Drive.

Beach Walking in San Diego County

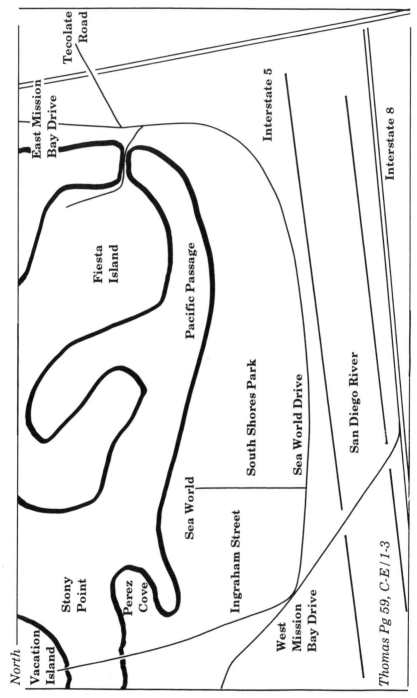

Beach Walking in San Diego County

Sea World
Fiesta Island
Mission Bay -South

Thomas Guide Page 59, C-E / 1-3

Tecolate Road (Sea World Drive) off Interstate 5 (*Pg 59, E / 1*) leads directly into this area of Mission Bay. Continue west onto Sea World Drive.

Fiesta Island (*Pg 59, D / 1*) is entered off Sea World Drive. This is a man-made island with plentiful parking, restrooms and sand beaches. It is more used for boating and water-skiing than for swimming. Walkways and paths are everywhere.

South Shores Park (*Pg 59, C-D / 2*) was under construction in 1992. It will have restrooms, a car lot and other park facilities. There is no public transportation to either of the above sites.

Sea World (*Pg 59, C / 2*) is a major San Diego attraction (Entry fee). There are large car lots, food services and entertainment features. Public transportation via SDT # 9. Schedules: 233-3004.

Perez Cove (*Pg 59, C / 1*) is a small park and terminal for the Sea World Sky Ride. A walkway leads under Ingraham Street to Dana Landing.

Sea World Drive ends at a confusing interchange (*Pg 59, C / 2*) which leads to Ingraham Street and Vacation Island; or to Mission Beach and Ocean Beach sand beaches via West Mission Bay Drive.

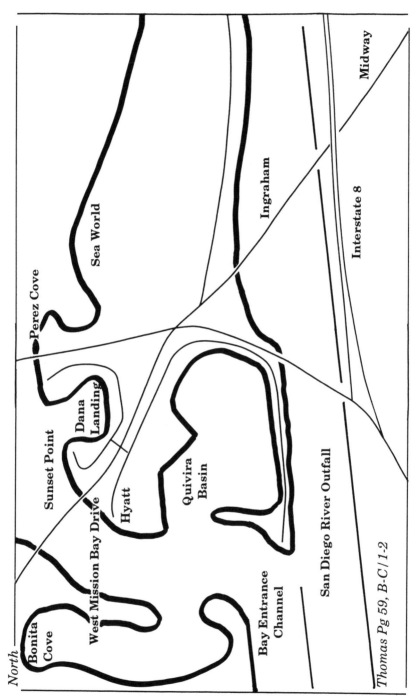

Beach Walking in San Diego County

Thomas Guide Pg 59, B-C/1-2

Quivira Basin Dana Landing

To reach this area of Mission Bay, take Interstate 8 west to the Midway exit (*Pg 59, D/3*). Turn right and watch right for the confusing interchange with directions to West Mission Bay Drive. Shortly after leaving the interchange a traffic signal controls the entrance to Dana Landing, Quivira Basin and the Hyatt Islandia Hotel. Public transit via SDT # 81. Schedules 233-3004.

For Sunset Point (Not mapped) turn right to Dana Landing Road, then left to the Sunset Point (*Pg 59, B/1*) carlot. There are restrooms, fire rings, picnic tables, grass, shade and paved walkways leading east and west. There is no water access.

Turn right into Dana Landing Road, and right again, to Dana Basin Launching ramps (*Pg 59, C/1*). There are restrooms, carlot, telephones and picnic tables. Boat launching water access only.

Further on there is Dana Landing (*Pg 59, C/1*) with a small carlot, grass, fire rings, picnic tables and telephone. A paved walk leads to Perez Cove.

For Quivira Basin (*Pg 59, B/2*) turn left off West Mission Bay Drive and left again onto Quivira Road. Continue ahead, curving right onto Quivira Way, to a grassed park, carlot, restrooms, fire rings, picnic tables, shade and telephones. There is no water access at this point. A jetty leads seaward and paved walkways lead north and east.

For the Hyatt Islandia area turn left off West Mission Bay Drive then right onto Quivira Road. There is a small park past the Islandia Hotel with grass, fire rings, picnic tables and telephone. A paved walkway leads to Perez Cove. No water access off the rip rap channel walls.

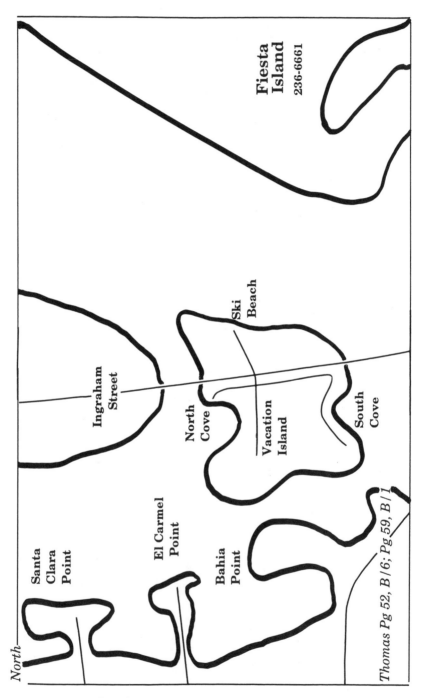

North

Santa
Clara
Point

El Carmel
Point

Bahia
Point

Ingraham
Street

North
Cove

Vacation
Island

Ski
Beach

South
Cove

Fiesta
Island
236-6661

Thomas Pg 52, B/6; Pg 59, B/1

Beach Walking in San Diego County

Thomas Guide Pg 52, B-C/6 and Pg 59, B-C/1

Ski Beach
Vacation Island

To reach this central portion of Mission Bay, take Interstate 8 West to the Midway exit (*Pg 59, D/3*). Go right to Ingraham, then continue ahead onto Vacation Road (*Pg 59, C/1*). Public transit via SDT # 9. Schedules: 233-3004.

Vacation Island (*Pg 52, B-C/6 and Pg 59, B-C/1*) is a private hotel surrounded by public beaches. Entrance directions on Vacation Road point to North Cove, South Cove and the Model Yacht Pool.

North Cove (*Pg 52, B/6*) has a car lot, rest rooms, fire rings, picnic tables, shade and sheltered sand beach for swimming. Beach walking is possible for one-half mile around the cove. A paved walkway leads under Ingraham to Ski Beach.

South Cove (*Pg 59, C/1*) is grassed parkland with rest rooms, picnic tables, shade trees and views of Mission Bay Channel. Swimming areas are marked. There are numerous carlots. A paved walkway leads west to Vacation Village housing and a sand beach with fire rings. The same walkway leads east under Ingraham Street to Ski Beach which does not permit swimming.

Ski Beach (*Pg 52, C/6*) is entered off Ingraham Street on Vacation Road. This is a restricted area for water skiing and boat launching. Swimming is not allowed. Carlots, restrooms, shade, grass, BBQs, picnic tables and telephones are in the Ski Beach area. There are paved walkways under Ingraham to north and south Cove beaches. Public transit is via SDT # 9. Schedules: 233-3004.

For Santa Clara Point, El Carmel Point, Bahia Point and Fiesta Island; please refer to the Index.

Beach Walking in San Diego County

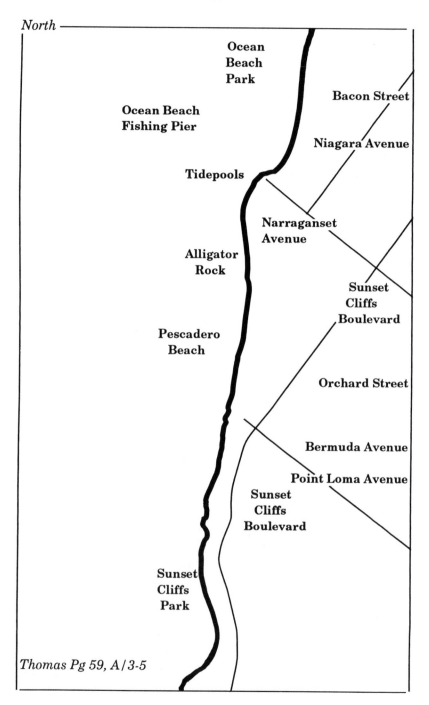

North

Ocean
Beach
Park

Bacon Street

Ocean Beach
Fishing Pier

Niagara Avenue

Tidepools

Narraganset
Avenue

Alligator
Rock

Sunset
Cliffs
Boulevard

Pescadero
Beach

Orchard Street

Bermuda Avenue

Point Loma Avenue

Sunset
Cliffs
Boulevard

Sunset
Cliffs
Park

Thomas Pg 59, A/3-5

Beach Walking in San Diego County

Thomas Guide Pg 59, A/3-5　　　　　　　**Ocean Beach**
Sunset Cliffs

To reach Ocean Beach (*Pg 59, B-C/4*) follow Interstate 8 West to the Sunset Cliffs Boulevard exit. Follow Sunset Cliffs into Ocean Beach. Turn right on any cross street to reach the ocean front. Public transit to this area is via SDT # 35. Schedules: 233-3004.

Ocean Beach Park (*Pg 59, A/3*) is a wide sand beach with restrooms, guard towers (Dial 911), fire rings and carlots. The area is noted for fine surfing. Beach walking is possible from Dog Beach on the north to the OB Fishing Pier, a distance of five-eighth mile. Food services and telephones are plentiful.

The Ocean Beach Fishing Pier (*Pg 59, A/3*) is near restrooms. A surfing area is north of the pier. The carlot is at Abbott and Newport Avenue. From here you can beach/path walk 12 miles north to La Jolla Shores Beach and Scripps Pier (*Pg 44, A/2*).

A tidepool area slightly south of the Pier (*Pg 59, A/4*) is not mapped. There is stairway access from Narraganset Avenue and a breakwater walkway both north and south. Street parking is scarce and use of the OB Pier parking lot is recommended.

This is a surfing area (*Pg 59, A/4*) with access via Orchard Street or Santa Cruz Ave. Scarce street parking. No facilities.

Pescadero Beach (*Pg 59, A/5*) is not mapped. Entry is by stairs from Bermuda or Point Loma Avenue and from Cable or Orchard Street. Street parking is scarce. No facilities.

Sunset Cliffs Park (*Pg 59, A/5-6*) is a strip of semi-natural park with limited beach access off the length of Sunset Cliffs Boulevard. 'Unstable Cliff' warning signs are frequent and should be heeded. There are no facilities and parking is scarce.

Beach Walking in San Diego County

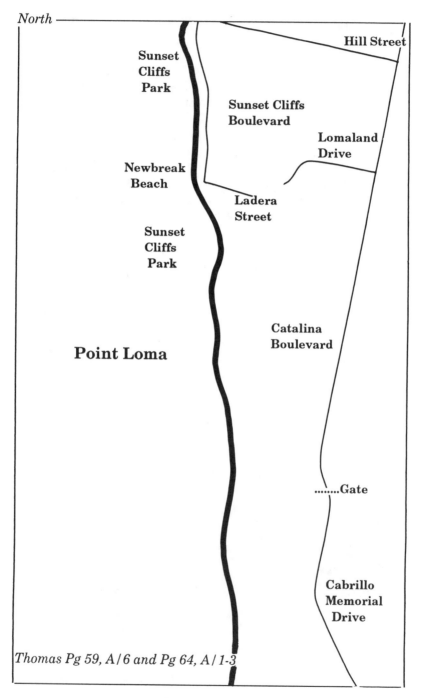

North ———

Hill Street

Sunset
Cliffs
Park

Sunset Cliffs
Boulevard

Lomaland
Drive

Newbreak
Beach

Ladera
Street

Sunset
Cliffs
Park

Catalina
Boulevard

Point Loma

........Gate

Cabrillo
Memorial
Drive

Thomas Pg 59, A / 6 and Pg 64, A / 1-3

Beach Walking in San Diego County

Thomas Guide Pg 59, A/6   **Sunset Cliffs Park**
and Pg 64, A/1-3   **Point Loma**

To reach this area from the North, leave Interstate 5 on the Rosecrans exit (*Pg 59, E/4 and D/5*). Follow Rosecrans to Talbot Street, turn right to Catalina Boulevard and then left. To reach this area from the South or East, use Interstate 8 West. Follow Nimitz Boulevard exit signs and continue on Nimitz (*Pg 59, C/4*) to Chatsworth Boulevard. Go right on Chatsworth to Catalina Boulevard and then left.

Sunset Cliffs Park (*Pg 59, A/6*) is strip park in which dangerous unstable cliffs are common. Beach access is limited along the length of Sunset Cliffs Boulevard. Few carlots and limited street parking. Public transit via SDT # 35. Schedules: 233-3004.

Sunset Cliffs Park has a rustic carlot at the intersection of Ladera Street and Cornish Drive (*Pg 64, A/1*). Portable restrooms and difficult beach access along random trails. There is a small sand beach and the rest is rocks. No other facilities. Some random walking paths in the area. No public transit.

Lomaland Drive (*Pg 64, B/1*) leads from Catalina Boulevard to the Point Loma Nazarene College. It is necessary to pass through the College gate to reach Sunset Cliffs Park between the college and sea shore. The gate guard provides directions to a carlot on coastal bluffs. There is a large playing field, random trails to Newbreak surfing beach but no facilities. A few walking trails exist. Public transit via SDT # 6. Schedules: 233-3004.

Catalina Boulevard is open at this gate from 0900 to 1715 daily.

Cabrillo Memorial Drive (*Pg 64, B/4-5*) leads to Cabrillo National Monument (Entry fee), a historic lighthouse and tidepools. The Monument is open daily from 0900 to 1715.

Beach Walking in San Diego County

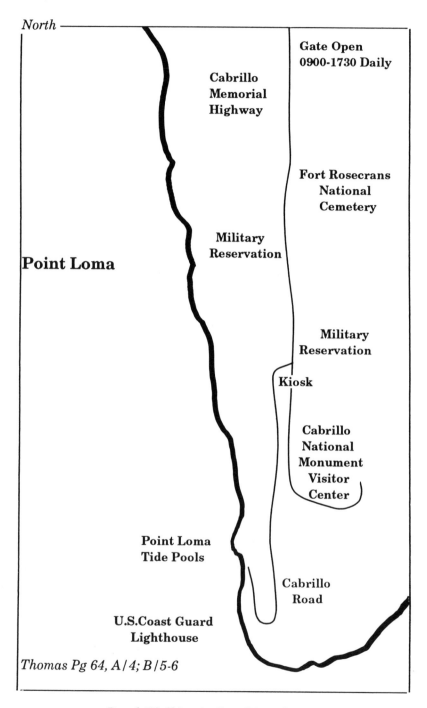

North

Point Loma

Gate Open
0900-1730 Daily

Cabrillo
Memorial
Highway

Fort Rosecrans
National
Cemetery

Military
Reservation

Military
Reservation

Kiosk

Cabrillo
National
Monument
Visitor
Center

Point Loma
Tide Pools

Cabrillo
Road

U.S. Coast Guard
Lighthouse

Thomas Pg 64, A/4; B/5-6

Beach Walking in San Diego County

Point Loma
Cabrillo National Monument

Catalina Boulevard (See preceding page.) changes to Cabrillo
Memorial Highway past the Fort Rosecrans National Cemetery
(*Pg 64, B/4*) after which it enters grounds of the Cabrillo National Monument which is open from 0900 to 1715 daily. Public
transit is via SDT # 6. Schedules: 233-3004.

Cabrillo National Monument (*Pg 64, B/6*) has a large parking
lot (Entry Fee), restrooms, snack services and a visitor information staff (557-5450). Walking is limited to a paved walkway to
the old lighthouse and Bayside Trail overlooking San Diego Bay.

Point Loma Tidepools (*Pg 64, B/6*) are at the lower end of
Cabrillo Road. The entrance point is about 200 feet north of the
Kiosk. The Ranger will provide directions. Walking down to the
tide pools is not recommended. There is a carlot, direction and
warning signs at this unique site. No ocean entry or facilities.

Beach Walking in San Diego County

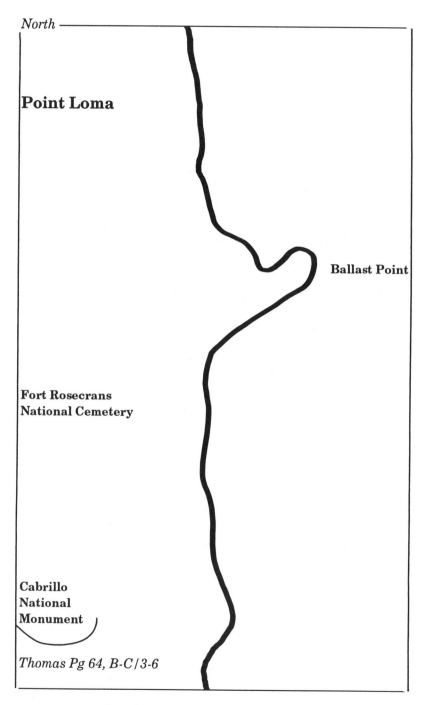

North

Point Loma

Ballast Point

**Fort Rosecrans
National Cemetery**

**Cabrillo
National
Monument**

Thomas Pg 64, B-C/3-6

Beach Walking in San Diego County

Thomas Guide Pg 64, B-C/3-6   **Point Loma - Bay Side**

This portion of Point Loma is a military reservation and public access is controlled. The entry gate on Catalina Boulevard is open from 0900 to 1715.

The Naval Submarine Base *(Pg 6, C/2)* has its main gate kiosk at the southern end of Rosecrans Street. Casual visitors to the Submarine Base (553-8643) are not allowed.

The Naval Oceans Systems Center *(Pg 64, B/3)* has its main gate on Catalina Boulevard. Casual visitors to the Systems Center (553-2717) are not allowed.

Fort Rosecrans National Cemetery *(Pg 64, B/4)* is open from 0900 to 1715 every day of the year. The entry gate is located on Cabrillo Memorial Drive. There are restrooms but no recreation facilities. For information telephone 553-2084. Public transit is via SDT # 6 and 6A. Schedules: 233-3004.

Ballast Point *Pg 64, C/5)* maintains the San Diego Bay Channel entry lighthouse.

Cabrillo National Monument *(Pg 64, B/6)* is open from 0900 to 1715 daily. See the preceding page for directions. Public transit via SDT # 6 and 6A. Schedules available from: 233-3004.

Beach Walking in San Diego County

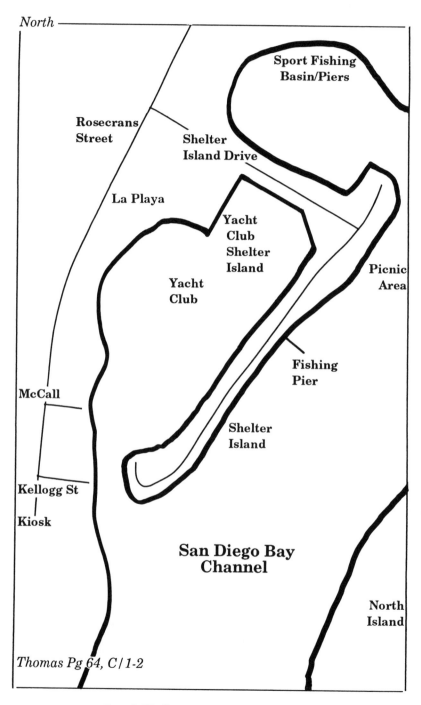

Beach Walking in San Diego County

Shelter Island

To reach this area from the North, leave Interstate 5 on the Rosecrans exit (*Pg 59, E/4 and D/5*). Follow Rosecrans to Shelter Island Drive. From the East, use Interstate 8 West and follow the Rosecrans Exit signs to the desired left turn. To reach this area from the South follow direction signs on Interstate 5 leading to San Diego's Lindbergh Field. Continue past the airport to Rosecrans Street, then left on Shelter Island Drive. Public transit is via SDT # 29. Schedules: 233-3004.

Shelter Island Drive (*Pg 64, C/1*) is entered off Rosecrans Street. The island has carlots, restrooms, water, grass, shade, fire rings, picnic tables and public telephones. Parkland on the Channel side has a 1.25-mile paved walkway. There is a small sand beach for swimming between the fishing pier and boat launching ramps. The land-side of Shelter Island is a marina with water access not permitted.

La Playa (Not mapped) is an unspoiled half-mile waterfront strip between the tip of Qualtrough Street (*Pg 64, B/1*) and the end of Talbot Street (*Pg 64, C/1*). There is a natural shaded walkway but no facilities. Street parking is scarce.

Kellogg Beach is between McCall and Kellogg Street (*Pg 64, B/2*) off Rosecrans Street. The tiny sand beach is without facilities. Street parking is limited. Beach walking is possible for a total of three blocks. It is an excellent spot from which to watch ships in the San Diego Bay Channel.

The Rosecrans Street kiosk is at northern limits of the Naval Submarine Base. Casual visitors are not allowed.

Beach Walking in San Diego County

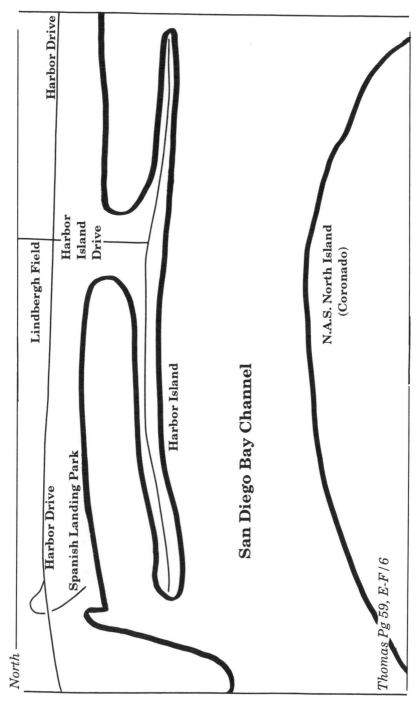

North

Harbor Drive

Lindbergh Field

Harbor Drive

Harbor Island Drive

Harbor Drive

Spanish Landing Park

Harbor Island

San Diego Bay Channel

N.A.S. North Island (Coronado)

Thomas Pg 59, E-F/6

Beach Walking in San Diego County

Harbor Island
Spanish Landing

Thomas Guide Pg 59,E-F/6

To reach this area follow signs on Interstate 5 leading to San Diego's Lindbergh Field. As you pass under the airport interchange on Harbor Drive (*Pg 59, F/5*) watch for an exit on the right leading to Harbor Island. Or continue past the Airport interchange and watch for a right turn exit to Spanish Landing Park (*Pg 59, E/6*). Public transit is via SDT # 2A. Schedules: 233-3004.

Spanish Landing Park (*Pg 59, E/6*) has four car lots, grass, shade, restrooms, water, picnic tables, telephones and small sand beach. From Spanish Landing there is a paved walkway, south along the Bay front, which can be followed five miles to near the 10th Avenue Commercial Pier.

Harbor Island (*Pg 59, E/6*) has limited streetside parking, a small car lot in the center, restrooms, water fountains, benches and some shade. There is a 1.6ml paved walkway the length of the island, a fishing pier and a sand beach. Major restaurants are located along this attractive site. Public transit is via SDT # 2A. Schedules: 233-3004.

Beach Walking in San Diego County

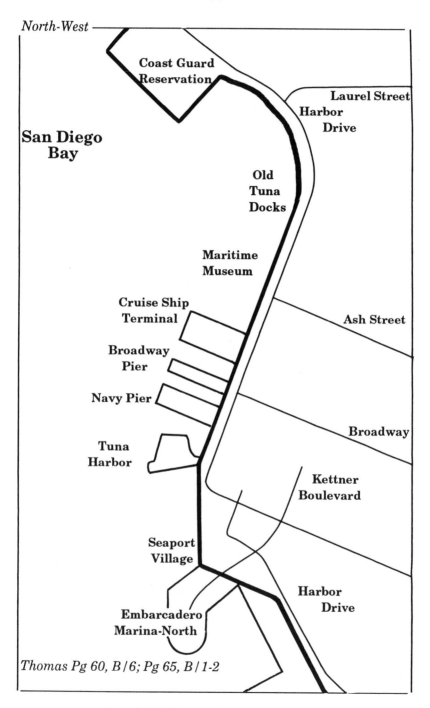

North-West

Coast Guard
Reservation

San Diego
Bay

Laurel Street
Harbor
Drive

Old
Tuna
Docks

Maritime
Museum

Cruise Ship
Terminal

Ash Street

Broadway
Pier

Navy Pier

Broadway

Tuna
Harbor

Kettner
Boulevard

Seaport
Village

Harbor
Drive

Embarcadero
Marina-North

Thomas Pg 60, B / 6; Pg 65, B / 1-2

Beach Walking in San Diego County

Thomas Guide Pg 60, B/6 **San Diego City Bayfront**
and Pg 65, B/1-2 **Seaport Village**

To reach this area, follow signs on Interstate 5 leading to
Lindbergh Field. From the South, follow Hawthorn Street (*Pg
60, B/6*) to the bayfront and turn left along Harbor Drive. From
the North, follow Laurel Street (*Pg 60, C/5*) toward the bay
front and watch for a left turn exit onto Harbor Drive.

Beginning with the old Tuna Fleet Docks (*Pg 60, B/6*), and continuing southward to the Embarcadero Marina, this area is a
walker's paradise. There are restrooms, water fountains,
telephones and benches at frequent intervals. The Maritime
Museum at Ash Street (*Pg 65, B/1*) has three unique vessels: A
huge sailing craft, a ferry and a delightful steam yacht. The
nearby Cruise Ship Terminal often has impressive vessels at
dock. The Broadway Pier (*Pg 65, B/1*) has metered parking,
restrooms and public telephones. Coronado Ferry and Harbor
Cruise ticket offices are adjacent. The Navy Pier is sometimes
open for warship tours. Inquire in Navy Command offices across
the street. Public transit via SDT # 2. Schedules: 233-3004.

Tuna Harbor (*Pg 65, B/2*) is a working harbor for vessels of the
American Tuna Boat Association. Enter off Harbor Drive. There
is a restaurant, fish market, metered parking, restrooms, grass,
shade, telephones, and picnic tables. It is also known as the G
Street Mole and G Street Harbor. Public transit for this and
areas which follow is via SDT # 7. Schedules: 233-3004.

There is a Seafood Market and visitor complex between Tuna
Harbor and Sea Port Village. Enter off Harbor Drive for metered
parking, rest rooms, telephones, shade, benches and fine food.

Seaport Village (*Pg 65, B/2*) is a complex of restaurants and
shops catering to San Diego visitors. Enter off Harbor Drive onto
Pacific Highway. Free and fee parking is available.

The Embarcadero Marina-North (*Pg 65, B/2*) protects a busy
marina full of expensive craft. Enter via Kettner Boulevard
through Seaport Village. The park has grass, shade, restrooms,
a paved perimeter walkway and metered parking.

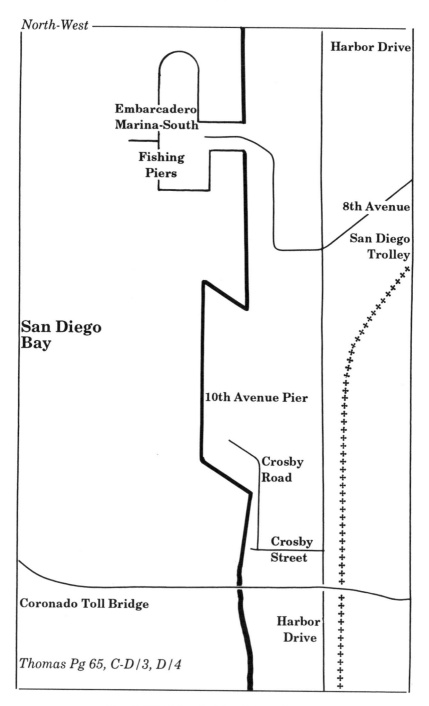

The best way to reach Harbor Drive (*Pg 65, C/2*) in this area is from Interstate 5. From the North use the Crosby/Logan Street exit (*Pg 65, E/2*) and go right on Crosby to Harbor Drive. From the South use the Crosby Street exit (*Pg 65, E/2*) and go left on Crosby to Harbor Drive. Turn left or right on Harbor to your destination. Public transit via SDT # 7. Schedules: 233-3004.

Embarcadero Marina-South (*Pg 65, C/2*) has metered parking, restrooms, grass, shade, picnic tables, telephones, fishing pier, snack bar, PAR Course and a paved walkway. Entry is off Harbor Drive onto 8th Avenue. There is a viewpoint for watching ship repairs in the Campbell dry dock and graving yard.

The five-mile walk from Spanish Landing Park ends here.

The 10th Avenue Pier (*Pg 65, D/3*) is a busy commercial pier and public visits are not encouraged. Entry off Harbor Drive is via Crosby Street. No public entry, transit or facilities.

Pedestrians are not allowed on the Coronado Toll Bridge.

Beach Walking in San Diego County

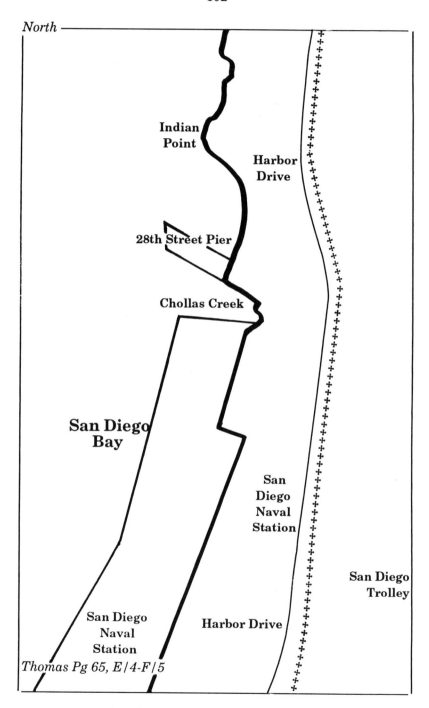

North

Indian
Point

Harbor
Drive

28th Street Pier

Chollas Creek

San Diego
Bay

San
Diego
Naval
Station

San Diego
Trolley

San Diego
Naval
Station

Harbor Drive

Thomas Pg 65, E/4-F/5

Beach Walking in San Diego County

Thomas Guide Pg 65, E/4-F/5 **San Diego Naval Station**

This area of San Diego Bay along Harbor Drive is the site of commercial shipbuilding activity. The 28th Street Pier (*Pg 65, E/4*) is a busy commercial shipping pier. No public access.

Naval Station San Diego's Main Gate is at 32nd Street and Harbor Drive (*Pg 65, F/5*). Public transit is via San Diego Trolley. Schedule information from 233-3004.

The Naval Station offers tours to the public on Tuesday, Thursday and Friday at 1000 and 1400 hours. For a reservation telephone 556-7356. The tour office, Building 3436, and parking lot are entered off the bay-side lanes of Harbor Drive. There is a sign 'Public Affairs Office' on the building. A parking lot signed 'Public Works - Visitor Parking' is not the tour lot.

Beach Walking in San Diego County

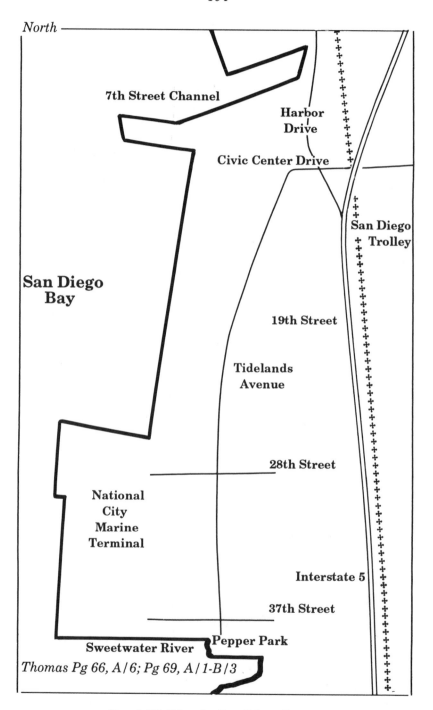

North

7th Street Channel

Harbor Drive

Civic Center Drive

San Diego Trolley

San Diego Bay

19th Street

Tidelands Avenue

28th Street

National City Marine Terminal

Interstate 5

37th Street

Pepper Park

Sweetwater River

Thomas Pg 66, A/6; Pg 69, A/1-B/3

Beach Walking in San Diego County

Thomas Guide **National City Marine Terminal**
Pg 66, A/6 and Pg 69, A/1-B/3 **Pepper Park**

To reach this area use the Civic Center Drive exit (*Pg 66, B/6*)
from Interstate 8. Go west to Tidelands Avenue and turn left.
There is no public transportation. This entire area is devoted to
marine freight and lumber storage. Public access is not invited.

The National City Marine Terminal (*Pg 69, A/2*), at the
waterfront end of 24th Street, is operated by the Port of San
Diego. There is an impressive complex of lumber storage yards
in this area. Public access is not invited.

The Mariner's Park (*Pg 69, A/3*) at the waterfront end of 32nd
Street is a wharf and warehouse facility. Not a public park.

Pepper Park (*Pg 69, B/3*) is at Tidelands Avenue and the Sweetwater River. This National City park (Open 0630-2230) has a
carlot, rest rooms, telephone, shade, picnic tables, grass and a
boat launching ramp. There is a paved walkway inside the park.
A short street named Goesno Place is on the east side.

Beach Walking in San Diego County

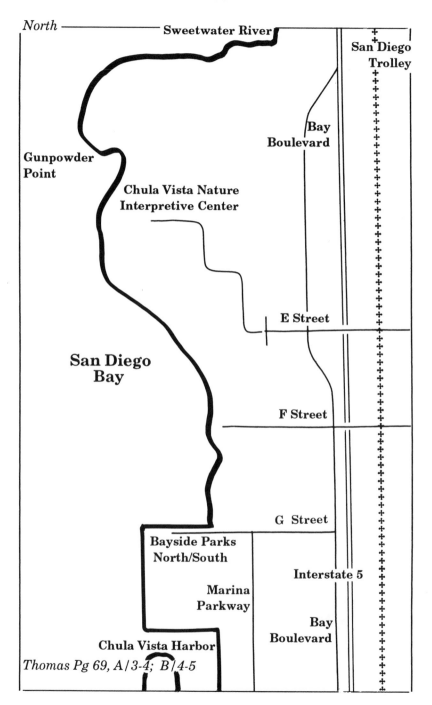

Beach Walking in San Diego County

Thomas Guide Pg 69,
A/3-4 and B/4-5

Chula Vista Nature Center
Bayside Park - North
Bayside Park - South

This area is reached off Interstate 5 via either the Bay Boulevard or E Street exits. Follow Bay Boulevard south to the desired destination. Or drive west on E Street to Bay Boulevard. There is no public transportation on Bay Boulevard.

The Chula Vista Nature Interpretive Center (*Pg 69, B/3*) has a carlot at the end of E Street. Public transit to this lot is via CVT # 701. Schedules from 233-3004. Transportation (Fee) from the car lot to the Center is every 20 minutes. The Center has restrooms, a bookstore and minor snack food.

There is a modest shipbuilding complex at the end of F Street but no public access to the Bay or recreational facilities.

Bayside Parks, North and South, (*Pg 69, B/5*) are reached off Bay Boulevard onto G Street or J Street. The later is an exit off Interstate 5 from which go west to Marina Parkway, then right. There is no public transit to this area. The parks (Open 0630-2230) have restrooms, picnic tables, showers, telephones, grass, shade, exercise equipment, sand beaches and carlots. There is a paved walkway through Bayside Park - South, to its fishing pier, which continues around the Chula Vista Marina Harbor to Marina View Park (*Pg 69, C/6*) on the south.

Beach Walking in San Diego County

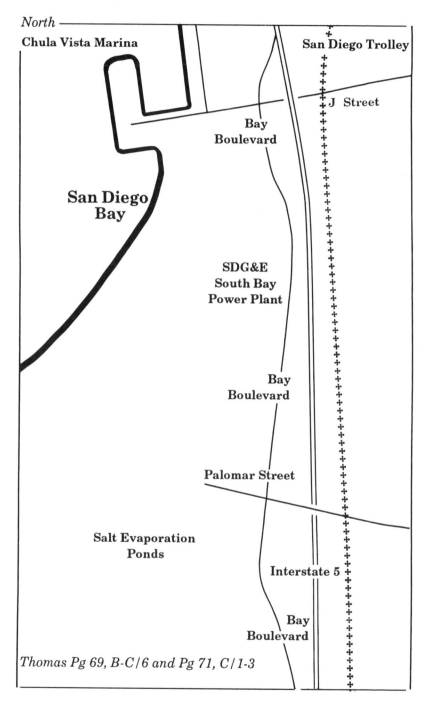

Beach Walking in San Diego County

Thomas Pg 69, B-C/6
and Pg 71, C/1-3

Chula Vista Marina
Salt Evaporation Ponds

The Chula Vista Marina (*Pg 69, B/5*) is reached by using the J Street exit from Interstate 5. Drive west and turn right onto Marina Parkway to the desired destination. There is no public transportation to this area. There is a club house, yacht club and extensive anchorage. Food, restrooms and telephone are in the clubhouse. A collection of carlots fronts the marina.

Marina View Park (*Pg 69, C/6*) extends into San Diego Bay and margins the bay side of Chula Vista Harbor. There are restrooms, telephones, picnic facilities and boat launching. A paved walkway connects Bayside and Marina View Parks.

The SDG&E South Bay Power Plant near L Street and Bay Boulevard (*Pg 69, D/6*) is an important part of the area power net. Visitor tours may be arranged by telephoning 696-4294.

This area of San Diego Bay and Bay Boulevard are accessed via the Palomar Street exit (*Pg 71, D/2*) off Interstate 5.

Salt evaporation ponds on Bay Boulevard at Belle Street (*Pg 71, A-B/1-3*) are a unique feature of San Diego Bay. They are operated by the Western Salt Company. Not open to the public.

Beach Walking in San Diego County

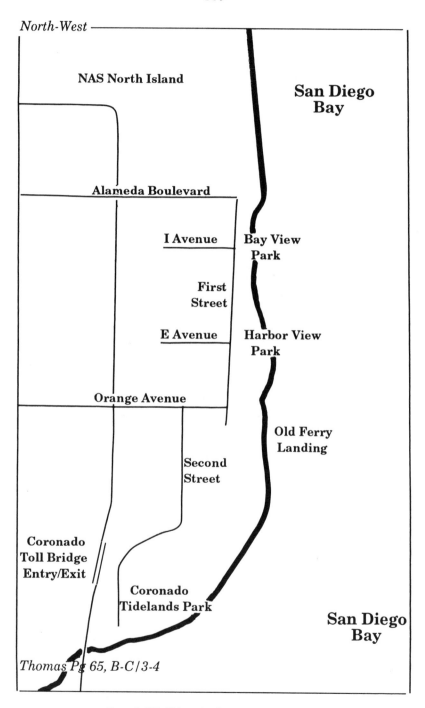

NAS North Island

San Diego
Bay

Alameda Boulevard

I Avenue

Bay View
Park

First
Street

E Avenue

Harbor View
Park

Orange Avenue

Old Ferry
Landing

Second
Street

Coronado
Toll Bridge
Entry/Exit

Coronado
Tidelands Park

San Diego
Bay

Thomas Pg 65, B-C/3-4

Beach Walking in San Diego County

**Coronado
NAS North Island**

To reach this area use the Coronado Toll Bridge exit from Interstate 5. After paying toll, continue ahead to Orange Avenue, then right to Second or First Streets. Public transit is by means of SDT # 19. Schedules from 233-3004.

NAS North Island (*Pg 64, E/3*) is not open to visitors. For information telephone 545-8167.

Bay View Park at First and E Street, and Harbor View Park (*Pg 65, B/3*) at First and I Street, are reached by turning left onto First Street from Orange Avenue. They are easements for utility lines from under the bay. Both have benches, shade and fine views of the city. Street parking. No facilities or water access.

The Old Ferry Landing (*Pg 65, B/3*) is a complex of boutique stores and food services. Benches, shade, restrooms and a fine harbor view. There are two car lots. No water access. Public transit via SDT # 19. Schedules from 233-3004.

Coronado Tidelands Park (*Pg 65, C/4*) is reached by turning right from Orange Avenue onto Second Street. At the end of Second, turn right again to Mullinix Drive and the Park entrance. Public transit via SDT # 19. Schedules from 233-3004.

Tidelands Park has restrooms, a PAR course, totlot, shade, grass, picnic tables, telephones and car lots. There is a small beach near the Toll Bridge. No guard service. A paved walkway leads under the Bridge to Coronado streets. In the other direction, the paved walkway skirts San Diego Bay to the Old Ferry Landing, Centennial Park and F Avenue (*Pg 65, B/3*).

Beach Walking in San Diego County

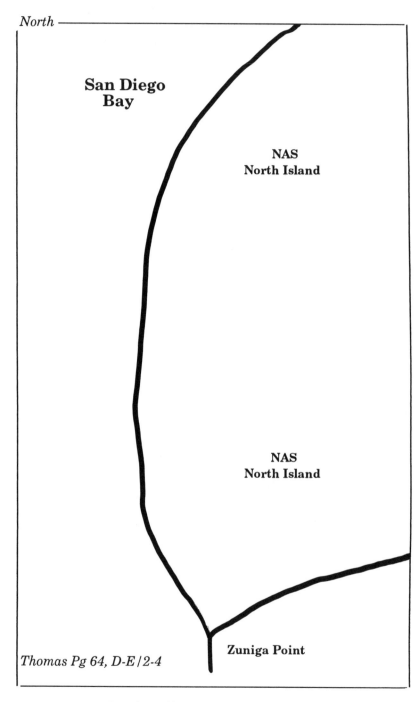

Beach Walking in San Diego County

NAS North Island is not open to public visits. For information telephone 545-8167.

Coronado's North Beach terminates at the waterfront fence located a short distance past the Navy's Gate 5 on Ocean Boulevard. This gate is adjacent to Sunset Park. The flight pattern of landing aircraft is over Coronado's public beach.

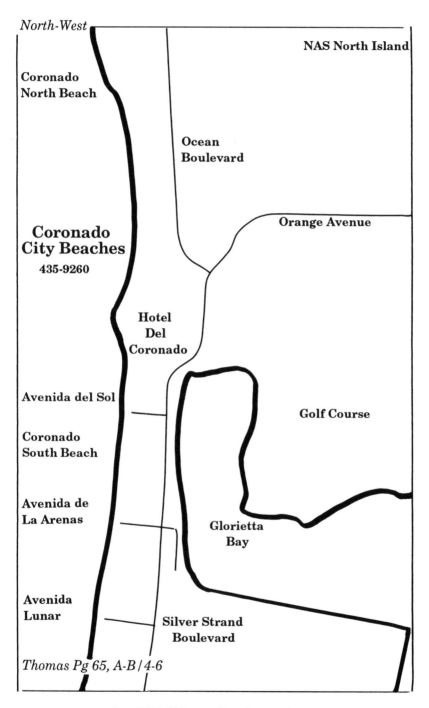

NAS North Island

Coronado
North Beach

Ocean
Boulevard

Orange Avenue

**Coronado
City Beaches**
435-9260

Hotel
Del
Coronado

Avenida del Sol

Golf Course

Coronado
South Beach

Avenida de
La Arenas

Glorietta
Bay

Avenida
Lunar

Silver Strand
Boulevard

Thomas Pg 65, A-B / 4-6

Beach Walking in San Diego County

Coronado is most easily reached by means of Coronado Toll
Bridge exits from Interstate 5. From the Toll Booth continue on
3rd Street to Orange Avenue and turn left to your destination.
Public transit via MTS # 901. Schedules from 233-3004.

Coronado's North Beach (*Pg 65, A/5*) is a wide sand beach between the Hotel Del Coronado and NAS North Island. There are
restrooms, showers, fire rings and guard towers. Street parking
is limited. Beach and path walking is possible north to fenced
limits of the NAS and south about 1.8 miles to SEAL training
beaches of the Naval Amphibious Base.

Off Ocean Boulevard at Churchill Place (*Pg 65, B/5*) is a paved
walkway (Open 0600-2200) leading around the Hotel Del
Coronado. Inside the fence is a restored 1905 bungalow used by
the Duchess of Windsor during her 1920 visit to Coronado.

Avenida del Sol (*Pg 65, B/5*) provides access to Coronado's
South Beach. The wide sand beach has a guard tower and ad-
jacent paved walkway. Street parking is limited but the Hotel
Del parking lot (Fee) is available. There are no facilities.

There is an excellent bayside park (*Pg 65, C/6*) on Glorietta Bay
off Strand Way at the Avenida de Las Arenas signal. Grass,
shade, picnic tables are adjacent to a 7.5ml paved bikeway.

Avenida de Las Arenas (*Pg 65, B/6*) ends in a small carlot with
ramp access to the beach. No facilities. A telephone is nearby.

Avenida Lunar (*Pg 65, B/6*) ends in a small carlot with access to
the wide sand beach. There are no facilities at this point. The
1.8ml paved walkway from North Beach ends here. Adjoining is
'Gator Beach used by the Navy for recreational purposes. This
area, and beaches south, are not open to the public.

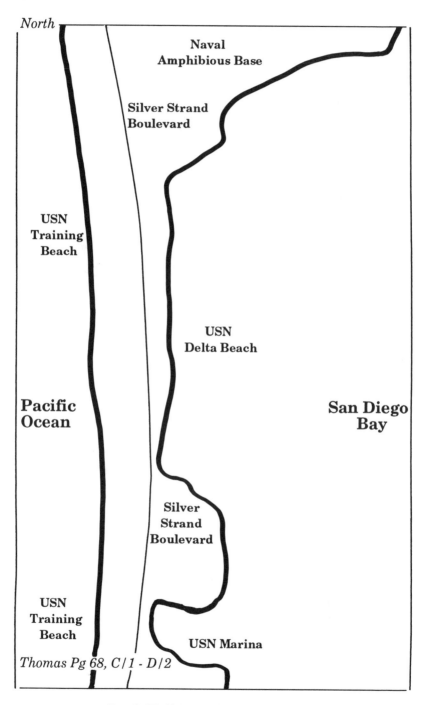

North

Naval
Amphibious Base

Silver Strand
Boulevard

USN
Training
Beach

USN
Delta Beach

Pacific
Ocean

San Diego
Bay

Silver
Strand
Boulevard

USN
Training
Beach

USN Marina

Thomas Pg 68, C / 1 - D / 2

Beach Walking in San Diego County

Thomas Guide Pg 68, C/1 - D/2 **USN Amphibious Base**

This area is most easily reached by means of Coronado Toll Bridge exits from Interstate 5. From the Toll Booth continue on 3rd Street to Orange Avenue and turn left. Follow Highway 75 signs to Silver Strand Boulevard. Public transit via MTS # 901. Schedules from 233-3004.

The Naval Amphibious Base (*Pg 65, C/6*) is not open to visitors. For information telephone 437-3024.

The USN Training Beach is not open to visitors. Please heed the frequent warning signs in the USN beach area. These beaches are used for training Navy SEALs under realistic conditions.

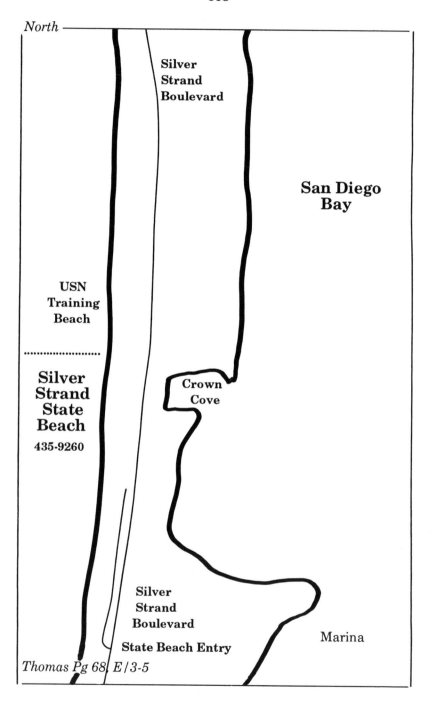

North ──────────────────────────────

Silver
Strand
Boulevard

**San Diego
Bay**

USN
Training
Beach

**Silver
Strand
State
Beach**

435-9260

Crown
Cove

**Silver
Strand
Boulevard**

State Beach Entry

Marina

Thomas Pg 68 E / 3-5

Beach Walking in San Diego County

Thomas Guide Pg 68, E / 3-5 **Silver Strand State Beach**

This area is most easily reached by leaving Interstate 5 on the Palm Avenue exit for Imperial Beach. Drive west then veer right onto Silver Strand Boulevard. Watch for the 'Silver Strand State Park' sign adjacent to a traffic control signal at Coronado Cays. Public transit via MTS # 901. Schedules from 233-3004.

The USN Training Beach is not open to visitors. Please heed the frequent warning signs in all USN beach areas.

Silver Strand State Beach/Park (*Pg 68, E / 5*) has large car lots (Fee), restrooms, fire rings, picnic tables and telephones. MTS Coach # 901 stops at the entry drive. Schedules from 233-3004. The wide sand beach has guard towers and is a well-known surfing area. Pedestrian tunnels under Silver Strand Boulevard lead to the Crown Cove bayside park (*Pg 68, E / 4*) with sand beach, restrooms, fire rings, BBQs and picnic tables. Adjoining is the 7.5ml paved bikeway between Coronado and Imperial Beach.

Beach Walking in San Diego County

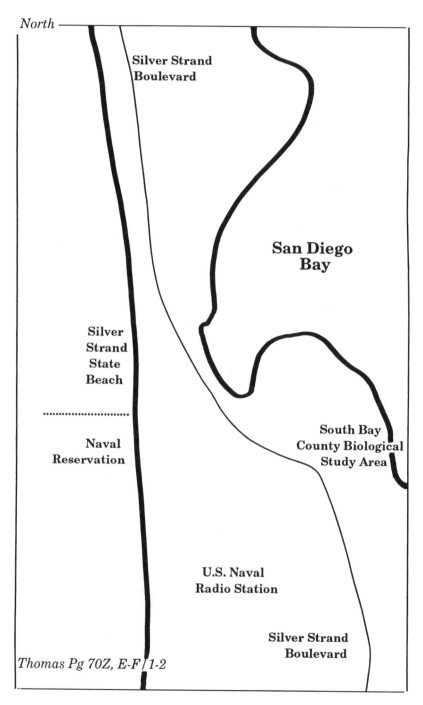

North

Silver Strand Boulevard

San Diego Bay

Silver Strand State Beach

Naval Reservation

South Bay County Biological Study Area

U.S. Naval Radio Station

Silver Strand Boulevard

Thomas Pg 70Z, E-F / 1-2

Beach Walking in San Diego County

Thomas Guide Pg 70Z,   **Silver Strand State Beach**
E-F/1-2   **South Bay Biological Study Area**

This area is most easily reached by leaving Interstate 5 on the
Palm Avenue exit for Imperial Beach. Drive west then veer right
onto Silver Strand Boulevard. Public transit via MTS # 901.
Schedules from233-3004.

Watch for a 'Silver Strand State Park' sign adjacent to a traffic
control signal at Coronado Cays. Public transit service via MTS
901. Schedules from 233-3004. Details on the preceding pages.

Signs for the South Bay County Biological Study Area (*Pg 70Z,
F/2*) lead into a carlot. There are no other facilities. The Study
Area is untouched tideland open for research and inspection.
Water access is not permitted. Adjacent is the walkable 7.5ml
paved bikeway between Coronado and Imperial Beach.

The U.S. Naval Radio Station (*Pg 70Z, F/3*) and its Naval
Reservation beach front are not open to visitors.

Beach Walking in San Diego County

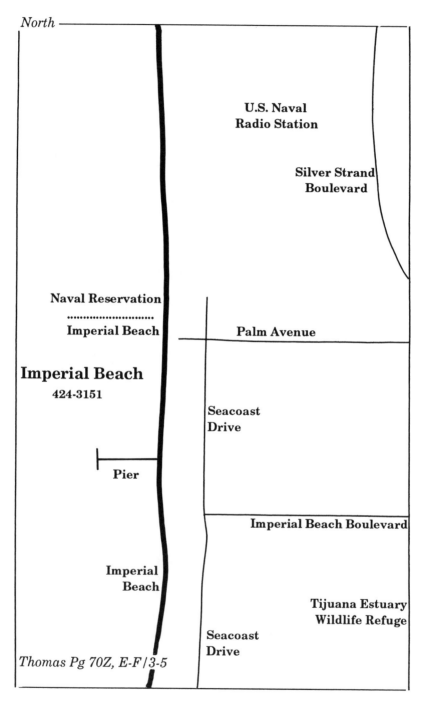

North ──────

U.S. Naval
Radio Station

Silver Strand
Boulevard

Naval Reservation
·····························
Imperial Beach

Imperial Beach
424-3151

Palm Avenue

Seacoast
Drive

Pier

Imperial Beach Boulevard

Imperial
Beach

Tijuana Estuary
Wildlife Refuge

Thomas Pg 70Z, E-F/3-5

Seacoast
Drive

Beach Walking in San Diego County

Thomas Guide Pg 70Z, E-F/3-5   **Imperial Beach
Tijuana Estuary
U.S. Naval Radio Station**

The U.S. Naval Radio Station site (*Pg 70Z, F/3*) is viewed by leaving Interstate 5 on the Palm Avenue exit for Imperial Beach. Drive west then veer right onto Silver Strand Boulevard. Public transit via MTS # 901. Schedules from 233-3004. The Station is not open to public visits. For information, telephone 437-9311.

Imperial Beach waterfronts are easily reached by leaving Interstate 5 on either the Palm Avenue (*Pg 71, D/4*) or Coronado Boulevard (*Pg 71, D/5*) exit. Drive west toward the coast and then right or left on Seacoast Drive to your destination.

At the waterfront end of Palm Avenue there is a wide sand beach with a guard tower, showers, rest room, telephone and a small jetty. Street parking is limited. There is beach access off Seacoast Drive between Palm and Imperial Beach Boulevard. The Imperial Beach Fishing Pier (*Pg 70Z, E/4*) is central to two wide sand beaches. It has a car lot (Fee), rest rooms, a guard tower, benches and telephones. It is possible to beach-walk .4ml north to the Naval Reservation boundary. It is also possible to beachwalk 3.5ml south to the international border with Mexico.

The Tijuana Estuary and Wildlife Refuge has a Visitor Center at 3rd Street and Caspian Way (*Pg 70Z, F/5*). It is open from 0700 to 1600 weekdays. There are restrooms. A visit is recommended.

Ocean entry south of Encanto (*Pg 70Z, E/5*) is deemed hazardous due to sewage contamination from the Tijuana River outfall.

Beach Walking in San Diego County

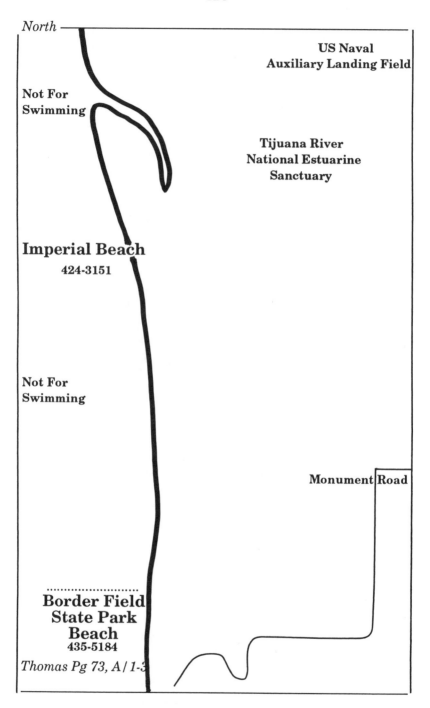

North

US Naval
Auxiliary Landing Field

Not For
Swimming

Tijuana River
National Estuarine
Sanctuary

Imperial Beach
424-3151

Not For
Swimming

Monument Road

**Border Field
State Park
Beach**
435-5184

Thomas Pg 73, A/1-3

Beach Walking in San Diego County

Thomas Guide Pg 73, A / 1-3   **Tijuana River**
Border Field State Park

To reach this area drive south on Interstate 5 and exit west onto
Dairy Mart Road (*Pg 73, F / 1*). Drive toward the ocean on the
rough winding road which joins Monument Road past the
Tijuana River bridge. There is no public transit or facilities.

The Pacific Ocean in this Imperial Beach area is deemed hazardous due to sewage contamination from the Tijuana River.
The final few hundred yards of beach are part of the State Park.

For information on the Tijuana National Estuarine Sanctuary
(*Pg 73, B / 2*) stop at the Visitor Center in Imperial Beach. See
the preceding page for directions.

Border Field State Park (*Pg 73, A3*) is at the waterfront end of
Monument Road. There is grass, some shade, BBQs, picnic
tables, restrooms and a carlot. It is closed Tuesday and Wednes-
day. There is no public transportation. The Park features a
monument marking establishment of a common frontier with
the Republic of Mexico on October 10, 1849. A fence separates
the two nations but Mexican swimmers and pedestrians ignore
the demarcation line. Do not cross into Mexico at this point as
authorities may insist that you walk six miles east to the San
Ysidro Border Crossing for return to the U.S. Entry into the
Pacific Ocean in this area is deemed hazardous due to sewage
contamination from the Tijuana River outfall.

Beach Walking in San Diego County

Index

Beach Walking in San Diego County